Canada: Origins and Options

THE FIRST CANADIANS

Canada: Origins and Options

THE FIRST CANADIANS

Author
Howard A. Doughty
Liberal Studies Division
Seneca College, Ontario

Consulting Authors:

Darrel R. Skidmore
Iain R. Munro

WILEY PUBLISHERS OF CANADA LIMITED
Toronto

To: Ralph V. Barrett and Scott O. Shields, who teach as much truth as can be known about the native people of Canada

Design and Illustration
KB Graphics

Canadian Cataloguing in Publication Data

Doughty, Howard A., 1945-
 The first canadians

(Canada, origins and options)

Includes index.
ISBN 0-471-99770-6

1. Indians of North America — Canada.
2. Eskimos — Canada. I. Title. II. Series.

E78.C2D69   971'.004'97   C78-001548-7

Printed and Bound in Canada
10 9 8 7 6 5 4 3 2 1

Cover photo: National Film Board of Canada

Foreword to the Series

During the nineteen-seventies students and teachers across Canada have displayed a growing interest in Canadian studies. This book is one in a series that has been designed to encourage the student of social studies to explore our culture and our heritage.

Each book in the series centres on one specific topic. However, all the books share some common objectives.

Their first task is to make Canada comprehensible to students. To accomplish this aim, each book concentrates on only one aspect of our complex society. Thus each book can provide a basic awareness of one set of issues that confront us, and the various options that are open to us.

The second objective is to help students use their basic knowledge to develop into politically aware and knowledgeable citizens. The challenges that confront Canadians today and will confront us in the future are difficult to understand. Only with a firm grasp of our heritage will we as individuals be able to respond creatively to the problems we will encounter in the final quarter of the twentieth century.

Finally, our hope is that this series will contribute to the well-being of our country by helping to create a more informed public. Any society, in order to survive, must be able to adapt to social change. Informed citizens are a necessary condition for any society which hopes to adapt successfully to the changes that are imposed by modern social development.

The conservative historian W. L. Morton once wrote that our experience as Canadians teaches us "that what is important is not to have triumphed but to have endured." Similarly, the poet Margaret Atwood commented that "Canadians are forever taking the national pulse like doctors at a sickbed: the aim is not to see whether the patient will live well but simply whether he will live at all."

If we are to live and to live well, we must begin to know ourselves. These books, we hope, will help to build such self-knowledge.

Howard A. Doughty
Iain R. Munro
Darrel R. Skidmore

Acknowledgements

Thanks are due to G. Hugh Duplisea, who read an early draft of this book; Dee Pennock, for her editorial assistance; and Jim Rogerson and Dan Lee, for their administrative support.

Howard A. Doughty

CONTENTS

Introduction

About ten years ago, many new voices began to be raised among the native people of Canada. They spoke with confidence and with hope. Sometimes they spoke with anger. What is important about these voices is that they have been heard. They have been listened to by other native people. And they have been listened to by non-native Canadians as well.

These are just three of the voices that broke a century of silence, of muffled protest, of weeping for a culture that had been bent but had never been broken.

Viola Haywahe spoke as an ambitious young native woman, seeking to improve her own lot and to improve the conditions of her people:

> I am young, and I am strong. I am proud of my heritage. Today I am preparing myself for a future full of hope and promise. I am climbing the ladder, learning all I can and taking every opportunity for my development. Education is my strongest tool against discouragement, my best weapon against ignorance, my shield against apathy.
>
> I accept the challenge of Indian leadership. I will help myself and my people. I have a part to play in the destiny of my nation.

Indian News, July, 1969

Fred Kelly spoke as Vice-President of the National Indian Brotherhood:

> There is an Indian uprising in Canada. It manifests itself in the Native Movement. It is ideological, social, legal, and political. Within the movement are a spectrum of views. One constituent is a militancy spreading like a prairie

grass fire. It is a re-enkindlement of a vision in which the destiny of the native people is in their hands. This revitalized quest for self-determination is to be pursued unswervingly with whatever means necessary. This is Red Power.

Toronto *Telegram*, September 27, 1969

Dave Courchene spoke directly to Queen Elizabeth II:

It is with sorrow we note that the promises of peace and harmony, of social advancement and equality of opportunity have not been realized by the Indian people. I am sure you will note on your visits to Indian communities that Indians have not, in effect, profited well from the prosperity of this great and wealthy nation. We are hopeful that Your Majesty's respresentatives will now, though belatedly, recognize the inequities of the past, and will take steps to redress the treatment of the Indian people.

Vancouver Province, August 12, 1970

Although it is dangerous to make generalizations about people, there are some things that can be said about the differences between the beliefs and attitudes of traditional native society and those of the modern European society that confronted it. Traditional native people had no notion of "conquering" nature; they tried to live in harmony with it. Unlike modern societies, native communities were based on family ties and religious obligations, not on individual achievement and competition. While some of the traditional values remain, the old societies have vanished. We must now ask: "Who, today, is a native person?"

Who Are the Native People?

Native people is a term that applies to all those persons who have descended from the original inhabitants of North America. They include Indians, Inuit, and people of mixed origins, many with partially European backgrounds. At the turn of the century, there were approximately a hundred thousand native people living in Canada. A quarter of a million were estimated to have been here when contact was first made with European explorers. Many of the native people suffered and died from disease, starvation, and warfare. In the twentieth century, the trend has reversed. It is presently estimated that there are more than one million native people in Canada, approximately 4.5 per cent of the population.

A Legal Definition?

About 270 000 native people are called *status Indians.* These are people who are officially recorded as Indians in Ottawa. They are normally members of specific bands and reserves. There are 565 Indian bands in Canada, and they occupy 2274 reserves.

In addition to the status Indians, there are about three-quarters of a million *non-status* Indians. A non-status Indian is a person who is descended from the original peoples but has not been recognized by the Government and so does not have rights or obligations under the Indian Act. The exact meaning and explanation of these terms will be presented in Chapter Three. For the moment, it is enough to remember that under the law it is not sufficient to be of native ancestry in order to be defined as an Indian.

If the law provides no satisfactory definition, where else can we turn?

A Common Culture?

Some people say that a native person is anyone who shares in a native cultural and linguistic heritage, no matter how the person might be defined by law. On the surface this may make sense. However, there are eleven Indian linguistic groups. Each one is divided into a number of variations, or dialects. The major language groups include:

Algonkin	(The Cree, Ojibway, Algonquin, Naskapi, Montagnais, Micmac, Malecite, and Passamaquoddy)
Athapaskan	(The Sekani, Beaver, Chipewyan, Yellowknife, Slave, Dogrib, Hare, Nahani, and Kutchin)
Iroquoian	(The Huron, Petun, Atiwandaronks, Mohawk, Oneida, Seneca, Onandaga, Cayuga, and Tuscarora)
Siouian	(The Sioux and Assiniboine)

Other groups include the Tlinkit, the Haida, the Tsimshian, the Salishan, the Kootenayan, and the Wakashan; they can all be found in what is now British Columbia.

There are, as well, many different sets of customs, religious beliefs, and forms of social organization. In fact, there is not now, nor has there ever been, a single group known as the "native people," in the sense of one large community sharing a common culture. There have been, instead, many different native peoples, each group with its own language, customs, beliefs, and forms of social organization. It is even incorrect to talk about native "tribes."

Some people, particularly the Iroquois and the native people of the West Coast, had sophisticated forms of government. They had councils which met and acted to make the rules for large and relatively complex societies. In fact, while by no means *modern*, traditional Iroquois society so impressed the leaders of the American Revolution that they carefully studied the arrangements of the Iroquois Confederacy before drawing up the Constitution of the United States.

On the other hand, there were many native people who lacked formal organization. They had smaller and more simple communities, with family units and clans but no over-all authority. They were a collection of small groups sharing the same language.

Without a common legal definition and without a common culture, there are only crude and imprecise ideas about who native people are. The only general thing that can be said is that native people are descendants of people who were here before the Europeans and were, despite the great differences among them, *the first Canadians.*

I am an Indian, and my aim, my joy, my pride is to sing the glories of my people.

Pauline Johnson

The Native People Today

Some things are certain about the native people. They are the single most dispossessed "ethnic group" in Canada today. Of the 74 800 status Indians in the labour force, only about 30 per cent are employed at any one time. Most native people are able to work fewer than six months per year, earning an average income of less than $2000. In fact, as recently as 1968, the Minister of Indian Affairs estimated that the per capita income of rural Indians was about $200 per year, an amount only slightly greater than the comparable earnings of rural native people in the three poorest countries in the Americas — Bolivia, Ecuador, and Guatemala. This history accounts for much of the anger expressed by young native people today. The following data are drawn from various government sources dating back no further than 1973.

Canadians	Native People	Other Canadians
Deaths per thousand	8.32	7.43
Infant deaths per thousand	62.12	15.3

- Native people in the urban areas average an unemployment rate of about 68 per cent.
- Native people who are not trained for skilled jobs amount to more than 90 per cent of the Indians in the work force.
- More than 10 per cent of native homes have only one room, with an average of 5.5 people living in each household.
- Ninety per cent of native homes average less than 45 sq. m of floor space.
- Sixty per cent of native homes do not have electricity.

- Forty-one per cent of all native people are on welfare.
- Four times as many native people die by homicide, suicide, and violent accidents as non-native Canadians.
- In the thirty-one years between 1944 and 1975, only 526 native people were graduated from universities in Canada — fewer than 17 per year.

How did this situation come to be? Can anything be done to bring about improvement? The first question can be answered in part in this book. The answer to the second question will depend very much on all of us, native and non-native people alike.

We Aren't That Different

Mostly I want to get across the fact that Indian people still exist, that we're contemporary people, that we have feelings and families, that we fall in love and have babies like everybody else, that we have language, mathematics, law, government, and more to say than "How" or "Ugh." I taught the Count how to count in Cree on *Sesame Street,* and millions of people realized for the first time that Indians have language and counting and mathematics. I taught Big Bird how to fry bread, and millions of people found out that Indian people have good things to eat — you know, they all figured that we were living on something very strange and weird before Columbus came.

Buffy Sainte-Marie, *Weekend Magazine,* January 14, 1978, p. 6

CHAPTER ONE

Traditional Native Values

Every society displays certain social values. Values are beliefs about the proper way to organize human behaviour. They may be thought of as a kind of social cement. As long as there is basic agreement about the goals and procedures that a society ought to have, social stability will result. However, if there is serious disagreement about social values, or if people are confused about social values, then it is possible that the society will disintegrate.

What Determines Our Values?

It is difficult to say what conditions produce specific social values. The variety of values among human communities is so great that it is sometimes hard to see any significant patterns at all. In some societies men dominate affairs, while in others women take a leading social role. In some societies the old people are treated with respect, while in others they are treated as a nuisance. Some societies encourage competition, while others are based on co-operation. Some people worship many gods; others worship a few; still others worship only one. There seem to be as many sets of values as there are human societies. Still, some basic patterns seem to exist.

To hunt the great bear, you must feel like a bear.

Niviaksiak

One important distinction can be made between the values of *traditional* societies and those of *modern* societies. Traditional societies are those in which the people live simple lives, produce only what they can consume, and rely on human labour rather than on technology to meet their needs. In modern societies, people live in very complex social environments. Economies are organized to produce vast wealth, and machines assume a larger and larger role in producing the goods and services that people enjoy.

However, this does not mean that the economic base of a society will explain all its social values. Societies with almost identical economies can demonstrate remarkably different family structures, religious beliefs, and ethical principles. Nevertheless, by examining the economic and technological character of societies, we can get a reasonable clue about the other social values that are likely to exist.

The Economy

Traditional economies tended to be *subsistence* economies. This means that the people hunted, fished, or raised crops for basic survival; but they did not produce more than they needed for physical well-being and the comforts of a simple life. There were toys for children, religious items, provisions for feasts, and a few luxuries. However, most of the work was directed toward satisfying the immediate needs for food and shelter. There was little or no saving and little trading for profit.

This kind of economy was common among native people. It resulted largely from the limited technology of the people. Since most native people lived off the land, there was little opportunity for storage. Hunting animals, gathering natural foods such as nuts or berries, and some small agricultural activities took the people's time. It was difficult to gain a living — particularly during the harsh winter months — and few communities could afford to allow their members to spend time doing things other than those necessary to support human life.

Sharing

The difficulties associated with earning a living in the wild resulted in an attitude towards wealth which differs markedly from the views of modern society. The idea that a person would want to enjoy private property was uncommon. The necessities imposed by the natural environment demanded that the people co-operate in order to ensure the survival of all. It simply made no sense for a hunter to protect the carcass of a dead animal and prevent its consumption by others. Without refrigerators, a moose or a caribou would rot before a single family could eat it. It made more sense to share. This was particularly true in view of the fact that the hunt was not always successful. Thus, one hunter's generosity today would be repaid another time when someone else was successful in obtaining food.

Sell land? As well sell air and water! The Great Spirit gave them to all in common.

Tecumseh

Conservation

Beyond the practical need to share in the work and the rewards of working, the traditional native societies displayed a respect for the environment that might be a lesson for us all. The natural ecology of much of Canada is fragile. Overhunting or overfishing can tip the balance of nature and result in the ruin of many species.

The native people understood the need to conserve game. This understanding took the form of a religious respect for the animals they killed. Thus, casually to toss aside the bones of a freshly eaten fish was not permitted. The spirits of the dead animals were to be appeased, and the remains of the animals were to be treated with reverence. It was considered immoral to kill more than could be used. As well, it was important to waste nothing. The animals that sustained the native people were the source of most of their wealth. Not only could the meat be eaten, but hides were used for clothing, sinews for binding, and bones for simple tools. To kill an animal and waste any part of it was an extremely serious offence.

The Family

In modern society, the family unit is commonly regarded as consisting of two parents and a few children. It usually also includes a small number of relatives, who may visit or get together at special events, but who do not normally live with the immediate family members or greatly affect their daily lives. This arrangement is called a *nuclear* family. It is a very modern way of organizing family life; it was rare among traditional people. Native families were *extended.* The family, or *kinship,* ties were much broader than in modern society. People were not intimately associated just with their parents and sisters and brothers. They saw themselves as members of a clan or tribal group that brought them into daily contact with many people, all of whom were regarded as "family."

The kinship system imposed obligations on all its members. Child care was largely a communal activity. The men and women were all responsible for the safety of the children, and all adults were expected to contribute equally to the work that had to be done.

Religion

Religion did not simply involve respect for the animals that were the means of livelihood. Religious beliefs went far beyond that. They influenced all aspects of traditional societies. The entire range of human activities was seen in the context of spiritual meaning. All of nature, along with all human society, was regarded as part of a spiritual unity. While the specific beliefs varied from group to group, it was a common feature of native societies to take religious practice more seriously than many people do today.

Art of the Pacific Northwest Coast Indian

Howard B. Roloff

The Canadian art form best known to the rest of the world is that of the West Coast Indians. For almost a century, it has been rated internationally as one of the richest and most powerful of all tribal arts. As early as the late eighteenth century, Haida and Kwakiutl artifacts were finding their way into European collections.

Great forests provided the media for the majority of the Pacific Northwest Indian artifacts. Cedar, fir, and hemlock trees were transformed into masks, boats, totems, dwellings, utensils, and clothes.

The coastline supplied the sites for their villages, and the sea yielded generous provisions of food. Such a fortunate combination of circumstances enabled the coastal tribes to avoid the hazardous trips of their inland brothers and furnished ample leisure for lavish displays of boldly carved, decorated artifacts.

Their cultural area includes the entire coastline of British Columbia. The extreme generosity of the environment and the almost mystical atmosphere of the shrouded coast probably influenced the

The McMichael Canadian Collection Kleinburg, Ontario

Tsimshian, Human Face Mask

The McMichael Canadian Collection Kleinburg, Ontario

Bella Coola Sisaok Head-Dress

In the old days the shamans could do everything.

Nakasuk

Religious values were associated with all aspects of human activity. The association between religion and medicine, for example, was very close.

social and religious complexities which evolved with the first inhabitants. Supernatural creatures were basic to their concept of origin. The people created an art form which celebrated and communicated this belief while illustrating their lineal descent and providing a visual reminder of acquired privileges or rights.

Traditional Medicine

"Their calling is a simple one, and consists in knowing the mysterious properties of a variety of plants, herbs, roots, and berries, which are revealed upon application for a fee. . . ." This is the description of traditional medical practitioners offered by a nineteenth-century observer. "Although these herbalists are aware that certain plants or roots will produce a specified effect upon the human system, they attribute the benefit to the fact that such remedies are distasteful or injurious to the demons which are present in the system."

It would be incorrect to call these ancient doctors "medicine men," since "many of these herbalists are found among women." As well, some people have looked upon these therapists as merely ambitious and greedy individuals. This opinion is expressed by many early commentators: "The traditions give . . . a certain class of ambitious men and women sufficient influence . . . to lead a comfortable life at the expense of the credulous."

A. Hoffman, "The Midewiwin or 'Grand Medicine Society' of the Ojibwa," *Seventh Annual Report*, Bureau of American Ethnology, 1885-86.

More accurate is the opinion that the shamans and the people both believed in the religious significance of the act of healing. This did not mean that they were unaware of the healing properties of the herbs, but that their explanation for their success was not merely physical. Indeed, "some of the rituals of the Seneca medicine societies such as the sprinkling of water to banish disease, and the chanting in unison of certain songs in language unintelligible even to the participants, are suggestive of certain practices of some of the Christian churches."

Virgil J. Vogel, *American Indian Medicine* (New York: Ballantine Books, 1973)

The Eskimos recognize no chiefs among themselves, considering every man the equal of every other.

K. Birket-Smith

An Integrated Society

The importance of religious beliefs, the idea of common property, and the broad definition of the family all account for the fact that traditional societies are *integrated* societies. There is no easy distinction to be made between religious practice, economic activity, and family obligations. The lines between church, business, and home are not clearly drawn.

Native societies did not divide up the lives of the people in the way that modern societies do. People lived together and performed all their activities in a stable communal environment.

From the point of view of modern society, this absence of change is seldom regarded as good. What would be worse, in the eyes of thoroughly modern people, would be the absence of our fierce expression of individualism. There may be no more telling phrase in our popular culture than that contemporary song title, "I Did It My Way."

For modern people, individuality and a sense of privacy are generally seen as good things. For traditional societies, these notions were rare and often dangerous. A person who wanted to be an individual could easily become a threat to the group. While each person was encouraged to develop skills, and was given the love of the community, no one was urged to behave in a way that would result in a separate identity from that which the community expected. Conformity to the values of the society was urgently required, and such conformity was rewarded with the approval of all concerned.

Decision-Making

Many modern people might well regard the lack of privacy and the limits on individualism as evidence of an unfree society. The values of traditional society might seem to them undemocratic. Yet it is possible to argue the opposite in some cases.

In modern democratic society decisions are made by politicians, who are supposed to represent the people. However, politicians come before the people mainly at election time. At other times, they act as they or their parties see fit. Citizen participation in decision-making is often limited to the active intervention of only a few influential people. As well, when we look at the organizations that control our lives, we notice that only politicians must face elections. Most others, including major civil servants and business leaders, never come before the public at all. At most, they are accountable to their administrative superiors or to their shareholders.

This kind of situation would not be tolerated in a traditional society. Because they were small and informal, there was ample opportunity for all members of the society to be consulted on every important issue. The leaders of native societies — the "chiefs" — were a mouthpiece for community opinion. At most council meetings the chiefs represented the general opinion of the clan or kinship group. The leaders who were prized were the ones with an ability to speak eloquently on behalf of the community, not people who desired to take action alone. For this reason, some traditional societies can be seen as being more fully democratic than modern ones.

Brother, if you white men murdered the Son of the Great Spirit, we Indians had nothing to do with it. If He had come among us, we would not have killed Him; we would have treated Him well.

Red Jacket, 1815

Pontiac in Council

Early Contact

Most people think about the contact between native and non-native society in terms of the devasting impact that the Europeans had on the traditional way of life. There is little attention paid to the gifts the native people gave the Europeans.

During the extremely cold winter of 1535-36, the French explorer Jacques Cartier was trapped in the ice of the St. Lawrence. He and the 110 sailors with him subsisted on food stored in their three ships. By mid-March 25 had died of scurvy, and the others, "only three or four excepted," were so ill that they had given up hope of recovery.

Then Cartier was visited by an Indian chief named Domagaia. When the Indian saw the condition of Cartier's men, he took immediate steps to save them. The native women collected the bark and leaves of a certain tree, which they then boiled and fed to the men. The native people had not heard of vitamin C. Still, their herbal remedy saved the French explorers.

It was not until two hundred years after that a surgeon in the British navy named James Lind read of this incident and began to experiment with dietary cures for scurvy. Until then, Europeans dismissed the native cures as superstitions and continued to believe that scurvy was caused by "bad air."

The Indians in the Yukon had another method of avoiding scurvy. When a moose was killed, the hunter's family each would eat a share of the adrenal glands and the wall of the second stomach. The Indians were getting vitamin C from the glands and organs. It was not until this century that modern science discovered that the adrenal glands are the richest source of vitamin C in all plant and animal tissues.

Values in Modern Society

There are marked differences between modern social values and those of traditional peoples. The values of modern society have been moulded by pressures that were exerted upon the tribes of Europe from ancient times. These pressures have worked to transform Europe and eventually the rest of the world.

Some people argue that traditional societies were societies in which time stood still. People did not write their histories. There were few great heroes or heroines. There were few great wars and battles. In North America, changes were slow and often imperceptible. It is generally agreed that native people inhabited North America at least twenty thousand years ago. Yet their societies remained much the same for thousands of years, until they encountered European explorers. Changes, of course, took place as people were forced to adapt to new conditions forced on them by the environment or other societies. However, changes were not planned as they are today.

Why was European history different? Why were Europeans more concerned with great leaders, national boundaries, and wars of every description? Why, indeed, did the Europeans "discover" Asia, Africa, Australia, and the Americas?

We can begin to understand the answers to these questions when we consider that the history of Europe was a history of constant crisis, a history in which war was glorified, a history born of tremendous stress and competition for basic survival. The competition and conflict that characterized Europe for many centuries did not come from any instinctive drive in Europeans to be warlike. They resulted from a struggle for survival on that small continent.

Europe, except for northern Scandinavia, is a most hospitable place to live. The climate is temperate. The winters are not severe. There are no jungles and no deserts to make life difficult for the people. Europe provided an environment for living that was well suited to human beings. Timber was plentiful for both houses and heating. Animals were in great abundance for hunting and domestication. There were fish in the surrounding waters, and the land was fertile for farming. Europe was a splendid place for populations to thrive and grow.

However, Europe was also a small place. Although resources were plentiful, they were not unlimited. Thus, when the natural population increase combined with waves of newcomers from the East, a pressure-cooker existence began to develop. Among the first examples of the problems that overpopulation would create was the fall of the Roman Empire. In the first few centuries after Christ, waves of immigrants entered Europe from the East in search of a better living. As people crowded in, the mass of population was such that the Romans were overwhelmed by numbers as much as by their own moral decay.

Survival in Europe could not depend upon a loose and spiritually satisfying life of co-operation and simplicity. It came to depend upon strength and discipline. Rigid social organization involving large numbers of people was essential if a group was not to be destroyed by its neighbours.

The period from the fall of Rome in 476 to the "discovery" of America in 1492 can conveniently be labelled the "Middle Ages." It was characterized by the ongoing struggle for survival on the densely populated continent of Europe. This struggle was marked by almost continuous warfare, and it resulted in the destruction of much that made Europe inviting. By the fifteenth century, most of the wild game had been hunted out and many of the great forests had been levelled. As cities began to grow, squalor and filth grew with them. For over three centuries, between 1347 and the 1660s, the bubonic plague came about every fifteen years and destroyed a large part of the population of Europe.

How were the Europeans to deal with this situation? Their first response was to guard jealously their own territories and try to expand onto their neighbours' land. This only resulted in a vicious circle. To be strong, it was necessary to grow, for there was obvious strength in numbers. However, the greater the size of a group, the more land it needed to survive. Thus it had to grow even larger. Since unlimited expansion in a limited area is impossible, something had to give way.

Some traditional European societies were simply wiped out. Others, such as the Swiss, used natural boundaries and fierce armies to build a protective wall around themselves. However, the solution to Europe's problems was found by people living on the western fringe of the continent — the Spanish, the Portuguese, the Dutch, the Belgians, the French, and the British. The answer they found was the "discovery" of "new worlds."

In North America, the Europeans found a way out of their difficulties. Irish, Danish, and possibly Portuguese fishing expeditions had come to the Grand Banks of Newfoundland long before the voyage of Columbus.

However, expeditions to North America grew to great proportions only in the sixteenth century. The cod fisheries provided Europe with a desperately needed source of nutritious food and offered relief to a starving people. In time, Europeans discovered that furs, timber, and cotton could also be taken from North America.

By the eighteenth and nineteenth centuries, the colonies were thought to be useful places for absorbing excess European population.

Population by Continent in 1650
(Estimated)

People per Square Kilometre

Europe	16.3
Asia	12.3
Africa	5.4
South America	1.3
North America	.1

Who Is Overcrowded Today?

People per Square Kilometre

Belgium	360.1
United Kingdom	241.4
India	183.5
Pakistan	81.6
United States	22.6
Kenya	22.0
Canada	2.3

John Cabot Sighting the New-Found Land, 1497

Public Archives of Canada

The poor, the restless, the criminals, and the lesser children of the nobility were exported to America, Africa, and Australia. The usefulness of North America to Europe has not diminished even in recent times. At the turn of this century, the central part of Canada was discovered to be a fine place for growing grain. Now Canada's resources are eagerly being sought by large corporations, and the northern part of Canada is under development for its oil and natural gas.

The only thing that stood in the way of massive expansion and dynamic growth of interest in America was the presence of the many peoples already living here. They were the *first Canadians*.

When the news of World War I reached Coronation Gulf, Ickpuck would not believe the western natives when they told him that the white men were killing each other like caribou. He pondered the matter for some time. Certainly, white men who deliberately used their extraordinary knowledge and powers for the wholesale massacre of each other were strangely unnatural and inhuman.

Diamond Jenness, *People of the Twilight*, quoted in Stanley B. Ryerson, *The Founding of Canada* (Toronto: Progress Books, 1975)

The values of the European societies clashed with traditional values. Europe, of course, had been the home of traditional peoples for all of pre-recorded history. However, the pressures that have been described resulted in either the transformation or the destruction of such people — except for the Laplanders, who are among the last traditional peoples of Europe. They live on the northern fringe of Scandinavia and are only now being confronted with the sort of social change that was imposed upon the native people of Canada as long as four hundred years ago.

What are the modern values that swept over Europe and the world? They include

- a belief in competition
- a belief in aggressive individualism
- a belief in science and technology
- a belief in conquering nature

Competition

European societies were forced to compete in order to survive. Co-operation was a luxury that no society could afford, or thought it could afford. Thus, it was no accident that Europeans came to think in terms of the "survival of the fittest."

Aggressive Individualism

By the sixteenth century, Europeans had lost most of the close family relationships common to traditional kinship relations. In modern times, the idea has become fashionable that everyone is in competition with everyone else. However, traditional people sometimes feel out of place in modern society, and people with modern values find it difficult to understand traditional people.

Perhaps the ideas of competition and individualism can best be explained by referring to a true story told by a contemporary native person, Walter Currie:

I remember visiting a classroom of Indian children. The "white" teacher called on one of them to answer a question, but the child did not give the correct answer. The teacher then asked another pupil. To the surprise of the teacher, not only did the second child say that she did not know the answer, but all the children replied in turn that they did not know as well.

*In the government you call civilized, the happiness of the people is
constantly sacrificed to the splendour of empire.*

Joseph Brant

The Great False Face

Bernhard Cinader

The creator met the giant fálse face leader
who claimed that he was the maker of the
earth. The creator challenged him to a
contest — who could move the mountain?

The great false face shook his turtle
rattle and summoned the mountain, but
the mountain moved only slightly. When
the creator gave the command, the
mountain obeyed and enormous heat was
generated. The great false face turned his
head. His face struck the mountain,
breaking his nose, and his mouth became
distorted by pain. As the heat of the
mountain threatened to suffocate him, he
struggled for air and his tongue was
drooping.

The creator told the great false face
that he would give him a place in the
rocky hills of the West, near the rim of
the earth. He assigned him to the tasks of
blowing sweet gentle air over the crops,
driving disease from the earth, and
assisting hunters and travellers.

The teacher was confused, for these were
bright and obedient children and it seemed
strange that they either were all poorly prepared
or else they were all defying the teacher and
purposely disrupting the class. It took some time
for the teacher to understand that these children
did not feel comfortable with a competitive
situation. If any of the children had answered a
question correctly, after another one had gotten
it wrong, the first child would have felt ashamed
and the second would have felt guilty for
embarrassing the first.

In some societies, however, people are only
too happy to prove that they are better than
their fellows.

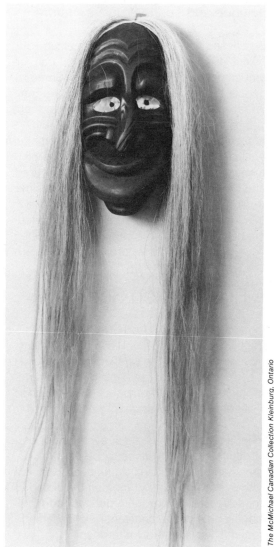

The McMichael Canadian Collection Kleinburg, Ontario

Broken Nose Mask

We have a word for the time before white people came. In your language it means: "the time when the earth was steady."

Anonymous

Science and Technology vs. Nature

Europeans have discovered that human beings are capable of inventions that can, or that can appear to, conquer nature. Some people today worry that nature may yet get its revenge. However, in the meantime, there seems to be little that scientific ideas and technological devices cannot do. With modern equipment, people can move mountains or tunnel through them. Diseases can be cured, and life can be prolonged. It is now possible to fly to the moon. For many native people, this technological universe that people have created for themselves shows only that they have lost respect for nature.

A Fragmented Society

In modern society, people live their lives in fragments, in small parts. They all play many different roles. In their relations with others, they react differently to parents, sisters and brothers, storekeepers, police officers, and teachers. They are seldom "whole" people.

This is not surprising, since many people meet and deal with dozens, even hundreds, of others every day. It would be next to impossible to have meaningful relationships with everyone. Think of the confusion and anger you would cause if you stopped for a lengthy chat with a check-out clerk at the supermarket on a busy afternoon.

In modern society, people travel freely and frequently. They change neighbourhoods and move from city to city. Most people today live some kilometres from their place of work. All these things make modern society different from traditional societies. In modern society, the institution of private property, the belief in individual competition, the division of labour into specialized jobs, and the very size of the massive cities make people what they are.

A Dynamic Society

In particular, modern societies are dynamic societies. Change takes place almost for the sake of change. Styles and fashions, means of travel, school curricula, political leaders, and even personal friends change and are expected to change. Growth and instability are regarded as normal. People try to cope; if they fail, they become casualties of society — mental patients, alcoholics and drug addicts, or possibly criminals.

Traditional people encountering a modern society face many difficulties. It is little wonder that they often become victims of the modern way of life.

Summary

Before contact with the Europeans, native people had lived in the Americas for many thousands of years. The native societies were very different from each other. The people spoke different languages and had different means of making their living. Their communities were organized in different ways, and their religion and arts varied considerably as well.

Nevertheless, the native people had some characteristics in common. Their societies were small in number, and the land was sparsely populated. With a few exceptions, they led a subsistence existence and had little to compare with the great inequalities of power and position that had begun to develop in Europe.

Most important, the native people had no technology of warfare to match the powerful Europeans who would one day come to America in search of wealth and land.

The Impact
of the Europeans

The effect that the Europeans had upon native people varied from people to people, and from time to time. At worst, the native people were hunted and killed for sport. Thus, the Beothuk Indians were exterminated in Newfoundland. At best, comfortable arrangements were created in which native and European lived in comparative harmony. More often than not, however, the native people suffered from the intrusion of the Europeans — sometimes immediately, sometimes in the long run. In this chapter, we will present three examples of the impact of European society on native life.

The Hurons

Perhaps the first tragedy in native-European relations came with the contact between the Hurons and the French. The Hurons lived in a part of Ontario that now is popular among summer vacationers and cottage-owners. Although the Hurons had occupied the land for generations, it took only about fifty years for them to be decimated by war and disease and to be scattered across the country.

The word *Huron* was not used by these people. In their own language, they were Wyendot. The word *Huron* is most probably a corruption of the French word *Huré,* meaning "savage" or, literally, "pig-face."

Prior to the contact with the French, the Hurons lived stable lives. They had developed some agricultural skill and grew crops such as beans, squash, and most importantly corn.

The men and women shared the work. The women planted and harvested crops, gathered firewood, and performed household duties. The men cleared the land for planting and supplemented the diet by hunting and fishing. Unlike most European societies at the time, the Hurons were a matrilineal society: that is, people traced their family lines through their mothers. The Huron social organization resulted from their concentrated population within a relatively small geographic area.

The major villages had fifty or more longhouses, each inhabited by eight to ten very closely related families. These families traced themselves back to a common female ancestor. Each family, or clan, had its own civil chief and war leader. The tribe was made up of a number of such clans, and the clan leaders served on the tribal council.

The Hurons were occasionally at "war" with neighbouring tribes. However, these wars were really more like feuds. They resulted in little loss of life in comparison with the wars of Europe. Moreover, these feuds were kept under control by conscious efforts to promote friendships through trade. Not only goods were exchanged. In fact, the Huron and other groups made it a practice to exchange people. A few individuals, often children, were exchanged between tribes and, later, between the French and the Indians. Naturally, a group would think twice before attacking another group which held their relatives as "hostages."

The first contact with the Hurons was made by Samuel de Champlain in 1610. Champlain quickly recognized that the Hurons could be important allies of the French. Their territory was crucial, because it stood on the route to the great fur-trapping areas of the Northwest.

As well, the Hurons had become important to the hunting societies that could be found on their borders. Often, when hunting was poor in winter, other Indian groups would appeal for aid from the Hurons and would trade meat and furs for corn. The importance of the Hurons led to Champlain's efforts to befriend them.

The Hurons were reluctant at first, for they distrusted the new arrivals in their land. However, with the help of the Algonkin leader Iroquet, friendly relations were finally established. The Hurons quickly learned the value of trade with the French. Metal tools and iron arrowheads were a great advantage. Iron axes made clearing the land easier than stone tools, and metal kettles greatly improved cooking.

The Hurons, at this time, numbered between twenty and thirty thousand. In a short while, a brisk and thriving trade was built up. The Hurons not only hunted beaver pelts for themselves but also expanded their trade north and west in order to amass more furs to pass on to the French. Nor did the Hurons limit themselves to collecting furs. Jesuit missionaries reported that, on at least one occasion, the French became reliant on Huron corn to save them from starvation in the winter.

Despite this co-operation, relations between the French and the Hurons were often strained. The Indians had few troubles with the French traders (coureurs de bois). They found it more difficult to accept the priests who sought to convert them to Christianity, although the missionary preaching, as far as it was understood, did not appear to present a challenge or an affront to the Huron way of life.

When we arrived in this country, the Indians were so numerous that it seemed they would grow into a vast population; but after they were baptized, God called them to Himself. ... It was perhaps His wise design to permit their death, lest they return to wickedness.

Marie Guyard, 1681

Traders Negotiating with Indians

Public Archives of Canada

Part of A PALISADED HURON-IROQUOIS VILLAGE

Creek↓

C.W.JEFFERYS

Entrance Gate

Corn Fields

C. W. Jefferys

In fact, there were usually more tensions between the traders and the priests than between either group and the Indians. The traders often refused to help the missionaries learn native languages. The missionaries were distressed at the undisciplined behaviour of the traders.

Reasonably good relations were maintained for some years. However, in 1635 the first disaster befell the Hurons. It is not possible to say for certain whether the Indians fell victim to measles or to smallpox, but it is certain that a great epidemic spread throughout Huronia. From 1635 to 1640, a disease that had been imported from Quebec City swept through the Indian villages. By 1640, more than half the Hurons were dead.

Not surprisingly, the Jesuits were blamed for the trouble. The Indians would see one of these stern men in black robes approach a household where people lay sick. The priest would administer "Last Rites," and people would die. The Hurons connected the visit of the missionaries with the death of their loved ones. Fear and anger spread as fast as the epidemic.

Some Hurons wanted to rise up and drive the priests away; others feared that, in doing so, they would lose the trade that they had come to depend upon. The matter was resolved in favour of continued co-operation with the priests, and the end of the epidemic marked the resolution of the dispute with the missionaries. However, in the same year, 1640, the second disaster began.

Both the Hurons and the Iroquois to the south had become involved in the fur trade. The Iroquois were allied with the English, and the Hurons with the French. As trade grew, the slaughter of the beaver increased until the animals were all but hunted out. The quest for new hunting ground began.

In Huronia, the people were split between those who had been converted to Christianity and those who remained loyal to their old customs. The split became particularly important to the political life of the Indians. Christian leaders voluntarily gave up their positions in the community, because leadership was closely associated with the ancient religions. As well, war parties were divided; the Christian and the traditional Hurons refused to fight together. These tensions spelled ruin for the Huron people.

In 1648, when the Seneca invaded Huron territory, the Hurons turned to the French for help. The French sent a few soldiers to spend the winter in Huronia, but the soldiers were told to return to Quebec in the spring of 1649. This they did, leaving the Hurons divided and defenceless. The Iroquois were heavily armed with English guns. They attacked in the spring and early summer of 1649. The French succeeded in making one last trading expedition to Huronia, and thirty *coureur de bois* scurried back to Quebec with about two and one-quarter metric tonnes of beaver pelts. By 1950, the Huron nation was no more.

Some surviving Hurons made their way towards Quebec. Others split up and joined in with any neighbouring tribes that would accept them. Still others appear to have made a long trek to the south, where their descendants now live in the state of Oklahoma. In the Huron story, we can see how contact with the Europeans brought wealth and prosperity in the short run, but within half a century led to disease, dissension, and military defeat.

The Plains Indians and the Buffalo

The native people of the great prairies depended upon the buffalo for their livelihood. For countless generations, they had hunted these animals with skill and daring. Yet they had never abused the buffalo herds. As a result, the numbers of buffalo (or bison) were never depleted. The native people lived, once again, in harmony with their surroundings.

The buffalo provided the native people with most of their needs. The skin, fur, bones, and sinews were valuable as well as the meat, which could be cooked and eaten or dried into pemmican and saved for a later time. The buffalo hunt was the most important activity for the native economy. It also formed the basis of most other social activities. In the summer, people would gather together for great religious celebrations. At such festivals, tests of courage and endurance would be undertaken by hunters and warriors, who would prove themselves in the rituals and then hunt the buffalo.

During the eighteenth and nineteenth centuries, the Europeans showed an increasing interest in the Middle West. The Hudson's Bay Company and the North-West Company competed with each other for control of the fur trade. As they expanded into the territory hunted by the various tribes of Plains Indians, the basis for conflict arose.

The Europeans attempted to persuade the native people to give up the buffalo hunt. They used trade goods including both inexpensive trinkets and more practical manufactured tools. They also used cheap liquor. The famous trader La Vérendrye put it this way:

> My object was to oblige them to hunt smaller animals, which they are not accustomed to do, and at the same time to get the women to take it up and also the children of from ten to twelve, who are quite capable of it.

The introduction of the fur trade led to many changes in native society. Gradually, the idea of private property and the profit motive was introduced. As well, alcohol was used to further upset the native community:

> Whiskey has destroyed a greater number of Indians than either war or disease. No barter took place between the Trader and the Indian without the first offering the other whiskey. The Trader, who looks at his own interest, is pitiless, and laughs at the misery and degradation of the Indian.

(R. McLachlan, *Indians* (Toronto: Longmans Green, 1959)

The European traders, with native companions, produced a unique society, a new nation — the Métis. Like their native ancestors, the Métis were skilled with horses and roamed across the plains in search of animals to hunt. Some took up agricultural

Buffalo on the Prairie

Public Archives of Canada

If the police had not come to this country, where would we all be now? Bad men and whiskey were killing us so fast that very few of us would be alive today.

Crowfoot, 1877

pursuits, but most preferred to remain free of such ties. As long as the Hudson's Bay Company was in charge of the territory, they remained relatively content.

However, soon after Confederation in 1867, the Government of Canada decided that it was important to take control of the land run by the Hudson's Bay Company. Accordingly, it entered into negotiations with the Company and began to arrange for the Canadian take-over of the Plains.

In time, the Indians and the Métis entered into armed struggle with government authorities. Shortly after the creation of the Dominion of Canada, the native people in Manitoba stood firm against the Government. The resolution of the Rebellion of 1869 was the admission of Manitoba to Canada as a province. The native people received guarantees of their lands and their language and customs.

However, the land was soon taken over and the native way of life was forced west. The people moved into the Saskatchewan territory. Many had resisted the lure of European goods. Many more had adapted themselves to the use of modern equipment, but they remained partly involved with the buffalo hunt.

The great tragedy came in the 1880s. Pressed by the expansion of the new Confederation, the native people found themselves removed from their traditional homelands. Then the buffalo failed to come.

The First Use of Horses

It is not known just when the Indians of the Canadian plains first obtained horses. The Spaniard Coronado introduced them to the Indians of the southern plains in 1541. The horse, with few carnivorous enemies and in a favourable climate, increased and spread rapidly. Stray and escaped horses formed wild herds. As soon as the southern Indians learned the usefulness of the horse, they made raiding expeditions to capture them; and the northern tribes procured horses from their southern acquaintances.

The Indians soon realized that the horse could carry burdens and haul loads. The owners could move freely, own more property, move more rapidly from place to place, and make long journeys. Hunting was easier. The horse became a medium of exchange.

Intertribal relations changed. Raiding parties set out to capture horses in order to prove their bravery. Raiding and the buffalo hunt rivaled each other in excitement and popularity. As horses and firearms became more readily available, fighting between the various tribes increased in scale and frequency. Glory, prestige, and the control of the buffalo migration routes were the principal objects.

Indians of the Prairies (Ottawa: Government of Canada, n.d.)

You do not see horses because we have eaten them. We have also eaten our dogs. That is what your work has done for me. I shall not be able to live by the good words that are told to me. You see me naked as I am.

Yellow Quilt, 1881

Wandering herds of buffalo had grazed the plains for centuries. However, the demand for meat occasioned by the American Civil War — as well as the fashionable blood sport of hunting for the sake of killing — had devasted the bison. The Canadian Indians depended on the same herds as did the native people living south of the border. Both groups of native people found that the incursion of Europeans had destroyed the entire basis of their societies in a very short time.

The native people were forced to capitulate. Some, like Crowfoot, tried to use diplomacy in an effort to win the best peace possible. Others, like Big Bear, took up arms. The second "Riel Rebellion" took place in

Crowfoot

Public Archives of Canada

Tell them our great thought is to resist being made Irishmen.

Louis Riel

Big Bear   *Public Archives of Canada*

Gabriel Dumont   *Public Archives of Canada*

1885. It was lost and its leaders were put down. Men like Gabriel Dumont, the military leader of the Métis and Indians, eventually joined a "Wild West Show." The spokesman for the Métis, Louis Riel, was hanged. The majority of native people resigned themselves to living on the reserves.

Unlike the Hurons, most native people survived the expansion of the modern interests into their land. However, a price of survival was often destitution, despair, and a sense of defeat. The native culture is only now awakening again.

If the Inuit could not change, they would no longer be.

George Swinton

The Inuit and Indians of the North

Three hundred years after the Hurons, another example of contact between traditional and modern societies is occurring. In 1965, oil exploration in the North was barely under way. The Northwest Territories was one of the last potential oil-bearing regions in Canada that had not been explored. Only a few discoveries had been made in the Territories, but companies like Imperial Oil saw the opportunities there and began to take advantage of them:

> You go north to get the jump on the 500 to 700 other companies seeking out prospective oil fields. . . . Imperial has cut itself a part of the action — about 14 million acres [56 702 sq. km] of exploration permits around the mouth and along both sides of the Mackenzie River.

Imperial Oil Review, Vol. XLIX, No. 5 (October, 1965)

Miller Services

For the northern native people, the end of their seclusion was near. Arctic petroleum is a resource that is currently considered invaluable to Canada and to the United States. Mr. Justice Thomas Berger recommended in 1977 that no pipeline be built along the Mackenzie River without extensive research into the social and environmental effects of such development. He also urged that native land claims be settled before any construction take place. Nonetheless, it is clear that the North will be developed and that it will be developed soon.

The people of the North call themselves the *Dene.* They resent the incursion of "white" society. They resent the fact that their lives have already been disrupted and that further changes will undoubtedly occur.

> We are speaking from experience when we protest and say that development . . . can only be supported on the condition that the native people first be assured economic, political, and cultural self-reliance. Without that assurance, destruction is inevitable.

George Manuel, "An Appeal from the Fourth World," *Canadian Forum* (November, 1976)

What do the native people propose? One example of the written demands now being made is the *Dene Declaration.* In July, 1975, the General Assembly of the Indian Brotherhood and Métis Association passed this statement of rights on behalf of the native people in the North.

Both the needs of native people and the maintenance of the ecology are important issues in the North. In the great gold rush of 1898, much of the Yukon was burned over. Now, willow and aspen appear and provide excellent moose browse. Still, the soil is mainly sterile, and regrowth is slow.

> The gold-seekers in the Klondike cut down the timber for a hundred miles [160.93 km] around Dawson, and this growth has not fully come back in the seventy years since they left.
> In the white man's enthusiasm for looting the land, little attention was paid to the harm that the environment suffered. Nothing has been done to repair the ravages of the gold-seekers.

Jim Lotz, *Northern Realities* (Toronto: New Press, 1972)

It may fairly be asked whether today's oil-seekers will behave more responsibly.

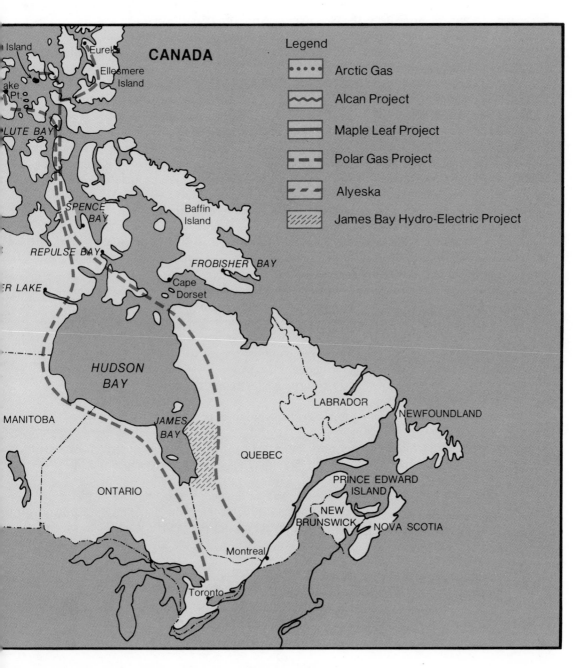

Energy Resource Extraction Projects and Proposals

Dene Declaration

We the Dene of the NWT insist on the right to be regarded by ourselves and the world as a nation.

Our struggle is for the recognition of the Dene Nation by the Government and people of Canada and the peoples and governments of the world.

As once Europe was the exclusive homeland of the European peoples, Africa the exclusive homeland of the African peoples, the New World, North and South America, was the exclusive homeland of Aboriginal peoples of the New World, the Amerindian and Inuit.

The New World like other parts of the world has suffered the experience of colonialism and imperialism. Other peoples have occupied the land — often with force — and foreign governments have imposed themselves on our people. Ancient civilizations and ways of life have been destroyed.

Colonialism and imperialism is now dead or dying. Recent years have witnessed the birth of new nations or rebirth of old nations out of the ashes of colonialism.

As Europe is the place where you will find European countries with European governments for European peoples, now also you will find in Africa and Asia the existence of African and Asian countries with African and Asian governments for the African and Asian peoples.

The African and Asian peoples — the peoples of the Third World — have fought for and won the right to self-determination, the right to recognition as distinct peoples and the recognition of themselves as nations.

But in the New World the native peoples have not fared so well. Even in countries in South America where the Native peoples are the vast majority of the population there is not one country which has an Amerindian government for the Amerindian peoples.

Nowhere in the New World have the Native peoples won the right to self-determination and the right to recognition by the world as a distinct people and as Nations.

While the Native people of Canada are a minority in their homeland, the Native people of the NWT, the Dene and the Inuit, are a majority of the population of the NWT.

The Dene find themselves as part of a country. That country is Canada. But the Government of Canada is not the government of the Dene. The Government of the NWT is not the government of the Dene. These governments were not the choice of the Dene, these were imposed upon the Dene.

What we the Dene are struggling for is the recognition of the Dene Nation by the governments and peoples of the world.

And while there are realities we are forced to submit to, such as the existence of a country called Canada, we insist on the right to self-determination as a distinct people and the recognition of the Dene Nation.

We the Dene are part of the Fourth World. And as the peoples and Nations of the world have come to recognize the existence and rights of those peoples who make up the Third Word the day must come and will come when the nations of the Fourth World will come to be recognized and respected. The challenge to the Dene and the world is to find the way for the recognition of the Dene Nation.

Our plea to the world is to help us in our struggle to find a place in the world community where we can exercise our right to self-determination as a distinct people and as a nation.

What we seek then is independence and self-determination within the country of Canada. This is what we mean when we call for a just land settlement for the Dene Nation.

Native Northerners

Peter J. Usher

The Berger Inquiry was the major northern event of the 1970s. For southerners it brought the issues of native rights, environmental protection, and the impact of big development bubbling up through the normal news diet of economic disarray, national disunity, and natural disasters. Judge Berger became something of a folk hero, and his two-volume report was a best-seller. For northerners the future seemed to hang in the balance. In the end, for the first time in Canadian history, a major development project was stopped, despite an earlier commitment to it by both Government and industry.

The legacy for Canada was a new approach to evaluating such projects, and demands for "Berger-style inquiries" have since been heard in northern Ontario, British Columbia, the Yukon, the eastern Arctic, and Saskatchewan. To many Canadians, all this is cause for satisfaction and a sense of accomplishment. But in the North the legacy is not so clear.

Despite Berger's clarion call for the settlement of native claims and the revitalization of native peoples' economy and society in the North, actual negotiations drag on with little progress. There are more books and more bureaucrats, and there may be more inquiries, but will they do much about the real concerns of native northerners? What are the real concerns, and what progress has southern Canada made in reordering its relations with the native people of the North? I believe that the true measure of such progress lies in the continuing policies of governments and their basis in public attitudes. . . .

Native people are concerned about the maintenance of their culture and way of life. Many southerners mistakenly suppose that because native people have adopted much of our material culture and no longer do all the things their forefathers did, they have forgotten their ways and values. In contrast, native people assert that their culture and way of life are very much alive. They express a strong desire to retain their values, their language, and their ways of doing things. Native people want to participate in Canadian society, but they do not want to be assimilated by it. . . .

Native northerners are not against change. They simply wish to control their land, communities, lives, and institutions. Therefore they seek measures that serve to maximize their autonomy and self-development, and to insulate their society from major developments such as pipelines. They want effective protection from such undesirable impacts as runaway inflation, disruptions in transport, communications and supply, and labour recruiting which leaves the small communities without the labour power and skills to maintain essential services and productive activities. Big development brings many speculative transients looking for work, as well as the usual assortment of carpetbaggers and adventurers who follow in the wake of all frontier development. Many native people have seen these invaders before and are not looking forward to their return.

Native people also say they must control the major public services such as education, health and alcohol programmes. Presently there is very little native involvement in the provision of these services. Native people fear that the impact of massive development will be, in the short run, to strain these services far beyond their capacity, and in the long run, through a changing balance of population, to place them in the permanent control of transients. The fear of becoming a minority in their own land is why native leaders have called for lengthy residence requirements for political participation in local and regional affairs. Native people also want the continuing power to negotiate on all social and economic developments affecting them, as equals. . . .

Another area of concern is economic development. Native people repeatedly assert the importance of hunting, fishing, and trapping in their lives. The economic importance of these activities is often underestimated by outsiders. In fact, most native people — even those who work full time — hunt and fish at certain times of the year, and their produce is a substantial proportion of their total income. That is why native people often refer to the land as their bank.

Native people need cash, and therefore jobs, but they want jobs and hunting, not jobs instead of hunting. When they look at the record of the wage economy they see that employment has been unsteady and insecure and that they have obtained mostly unskilled, low-paying jobs. Very few native people have benefited from business opportunities. They have had no share of profits from development and no control over government or industry investment.

Native people do not want to be dependent on one outside-controlled industry that will eventually go away. They do not want to become a mobile labour pool to be sent here and there as corporate resource development projects demand, for then the fabric of community life and the traditional economy will surely be destroyed. Accordingly, the bulk of native employment must be community based and community controlled. This means there must be smaller scale, locally controlled enterprises which produce for local needs as well as outside ones. The traditional activities must grow and prosper and be an integral part of the North's economic future. ...

Finally there is the matter of the involvement of native people in the future development of the North. The past record of "consultation" has not been good from native peoples' point of view. Development planning has usually been characterized by government or industry officials arriving (often together) at community meetings to tell native people about their plans. Native people have learned that these people come to talk, not listen, and that any opposition to their plans is in vain because the response is either that there won't be any adverse consequences or that these officials are not responsible for them. Such meetings have come to be characterized by apathy, which is eagerly interpreted by the visitors as mute assent.

Native people insist the old process must be changed; they must define a new process and be involved from the beginning as equals. ...

The past cannot be undone, and the Government cannot now pretend to start with a clean slate. But the future could be made different.

Summary

Each native community encountered the European civilization in its turn. Frequently, the results of this meeting were disastrous for the native people involved. Often the newcomers were greeted warmly, and trade with Europe was welcomed. However, the arrival of European culture inevitably meant great change. Some native people were able to adapt to the new ways. However, others did not have time or were not permitted to come to terms with the Europeans.

Disease, war, and starvation faced many native communities as the English, the French, and others entered native lands. In many ways, the pattern has been the same no matter when or where contact has occurred. The differences among the Huron in the 1640s, the Métis in the 1880s, and the native people of the North today are many; but the challenges they faced or are facing are similar.

CHAPTER THREE

The Legal Status of Native People

On August 8, 1969, Prime Minister Pierre Trudeau made a very curious statement about native rights in Canada. He said:

> It's inconceivable, I think, that in a given society one section of the society have a treaty with the other section of society. . . . [Indians] should become Canadians as all other Canadians; and if they are prosperous and wealthy, they will be treated like the prosperous and wealthy . . . and this is the only basis on which I can see our society can develop as equals.
>
> But "aboriginal rights" — this really means saying, "We were here before you. You came and took the land from us, and perhaps you cheated us by giving some worthless things in return for vast expanses of land, and we want to re-open this question. We want you to preserve our aboriginal legal rights and to restore them to us."
>
> And our answer . . . our answer is, "No."

The Prime Minister was no doubt expressing the opinion of some Canadians, but it is not possible to dispose of aboriginal legal rights just because they are inconvenient. They are part of the law of our country.

The Early History of Aboriginal Rights

Aboriginal legal rights originated in church law during the sixteenth century. In 1537 Pope Paul III issued his famous Papal Bull entitled *Sublimus Deus*.

The Pope declared that Indians had souls and were not mere animals, but "men." He added that Indians "may and should freely and legitimately enjoy their liberty and the possession of their property; nor should they be in any way enslaved; should the contrary happen, it shall be null and of no effect."

Equal Justice for Natives?

In those days, church law stood beside the law of the state and was of roughly equal importance. Thus, native rights were clearly recognized by the Europeans almost five hundred years ago.

In British North America, the Pope's ruling was accepted. Thus, in 1633, the British colony of Massachusetts passed a law in which it was declared that "what lands any of the Indians in this jurisdiction have possessed and improved, by subduing the same, they have a just right unto." In the colony of Virginia, in 1657, the government stated that "all the Indians of this colony shall and may hold and keep those seats of land which they now have, and ... no person or persons whatsoever be suffered to entrench or plant upon such places as the Indians claim or desire."

In the territory now known as Canada, similar statements were made shortly after New France fell to the English. The Proclamation Act of 1763 stated:

> We do hereby strictly forbid, on Pain of our Displeasure, all our loving Subjects from making any Purchases or Settlements whatever, or taking Possession of any of the Lands reserved [for Indians].

With that affirmation, King George III made aboriginal legal rights a part of the constitution of Canada. As one Canadian court ruling put it:

> This proclamation has been spoken of as the "Charter of Indian Rights." Like so many great charters in English history, it does not create rights but rather affirms old rights. The Indians and Eskimos had their aboriginal rights, and English law has always recognized these rights.

Aboriginal Rights since Confederation

Many more examples of the affirmation of aboriginal legal rights could be quoted. They all make the same case. Well before Canada was a Dominion, the right of Indians to their land was respected — at least in law. After Confederation, there is a long list of important affirmations of aboriginal rights as well. All these and many more examples would appear to put the matter to rest. Native people have, or did have, a clear right to the land.

Affirmations of Aboriginal Rights

1869-1870	When Canada purchased the lands held by the Hudson's Bay Company, the Government of Canada accepted responsibility for any claims made by the Indians for compensation.
1870	The *Manitoba Act,* under which Manitoba became a province, included provisions that land be granted to settle the Métis land claims.
1871-1923	The numbered treaties with many native groups were signed. In each case, it is stated that the Indians are giving up their rights to the land; thus, the Government was clearly acknowledging that the native people had such rights in the first place.

I am not here to dispense justice; I am here to dispose of this case according to the laws. Whether or not this is justice is a matter for the legislature to determine.

Sir Thomas W. Taylor

What Aboriginal Rights Are

Aboriginal rights are different from any other rights enjoyed by Canadians. Aboriginal legal rights may be defined as the legal claim that native people have in the land that they and their ancestors have used, and used "extensively," over long periods of time.

If this right is put in jeopardy by others (whether they be early explorers or the modern James Bay Power Corporation), the native peoples can advance a claim for compensation and even put a stop to the intrusion. They can do this if they can prove: (1) that they occupied the land for generation upon generation, and (2) that they used the land — for hunting, fishing, or farming — extensively during that time. If the proofs stand, the native peoples are said to have a right to the land. Thus, the land can be taken only by the Crown, which is to say, the Government of Canada.

Aboriginal legal rights can be taken away, or "extinguished," by three methods. The first is *conquest*. However, this is not applicable to Canada, because the native people were not conquered by force of arms.

The second method is federal government *legislation*. If this method is used, there need be no compensation paid to the native peoples.

Most common, however, is the third method, *treaty*. In truth, the treaties that have been signed by the native peoples and the Government are not treaties at all. They are contracts. As such, they require that something be exchanged for native lands. In our history, the contracts, or treaties, have usually seen vast tracts of native land given over to the Crown in exchange for a much smaller piece of land, called a "reserve," and often some money or goods.

Adapted from Scott O. Shields, "The Political Economy of Native Rights in Canada" (Reprinted with permission of the author)

Even if the legal claims are disputed, there is a good moral case to be made for dealing fairly with the native people. There are, for example, about 15 000 Inuit living in the Northwest Territories. They occupy and use 3 188 283 sq. km of land and water. These lands are now threatened by oil and natural gas exploration and hydro-electric projects. As the development of the North proceeds, the Inuit will be less and less able to make a living in the traditional way. The Inuit will not only lose their land but, just as important, they will lose a way of life.

The Inuit's Claim

There are immense social and human costs associated with the change from the traditional society to the new industrial society of the North. It is simply unfair for the native people to bear the brunt of the social costs of change. As the first and continuing land-users, the Inuit have a claim on a moral basis to benefit through non-renewable resource development as it comes to the Arctic, particularly because there will be tremendous social costs to them.

Peter A. Cumming. *Canada: Native Land Rights and Northern Development* (Copenhagen, Denmark: IWGIA, 1977). p. 28

Aboriginal Rights in the 1970s

Despite the evidence in favour of aboriginal rights, and despite the moral claims that can be made on behalf of native people, the fact is that aboriginal rights are now in jeopardy.

The 1970s began with some concerns by native people. Prime Minister Trudeau's remarks, combined with a government "White Paper," indicate that the Government would like to set aside all aboriginal legal rights.

It may well have been these statements that prompted the Nishga Indians of the Nass Valley to do something about their rights. They went to court and asked the judge to declare that they did indeed have aboriginal rights to their British Columbia homeland. Expert witnesses testified that the Nishga Indians had occupied the land since "time immemorial" and had used the valley "extensively." Moreover, the Nishgas had never entered into a treaty to sign away their land. However, in a surprising decision, the court ruled that they had no rights to the land.

The Indians, of course, appealed to the Supreme Court. After some years and the expenditure of much money, the Nishgas lost their appeal on a legal technicality. This case has worried many native people. With their rights in doubt for the first time, some have been eager to sign treaties with the Government for a small fraction of the value of their land. The Cree of James Bay, for example, gave up claims to much of Quebec in return for less than one and a half per cent of their ancestral homeland and a cash settlement that works out to only a few thousand dollars a person.

Whoever heard of a powerless and oppressed people re-re-negotiating the terms of their oppression with their oppressors?

Scott Shields, 1978

Supreme Court of Canada: Will Its Support for Native Rights Grow?

Miller Services

Presently, the native people are disenchanted with the courts. The Nishga case, the James Bay settlement, and the desire of the Government and large business corporations to develop the North have made the settlement of aboriginal rights a highly political issue. Recent inquiries by jurists such as Judge Thomas Berger into planned pipelines have given some hope to the native people. However, it is not realistic to hope for a great deal.

Treaty Settlements

When the French lost New France to the English, the document whereby Montreal was given over to British control stated in part that "the Indian Allies of His Most Christian Majesty shall be maintained in the lands they inhabit, if they choose to reside there; they shall not be molested on any pretence whatsoever, for having carried arms and served his Most Christian Majesty; they shall have liberty of religion, and shall keep their missionaries."

The British not only acknowledged the rights of native people to the land, but they also said that they would respect native culture. Unfortunately, this attitude did not last long. By the early part of the nineteenth century, the native people were regarded as being in the way of development. In 1836, for example, Sir Francis Bond Head, the Lieutenant-Governor of Upper Canada, decided that it would be best to remove the Indians from parts of what is now southern Ontario so that room could be made for

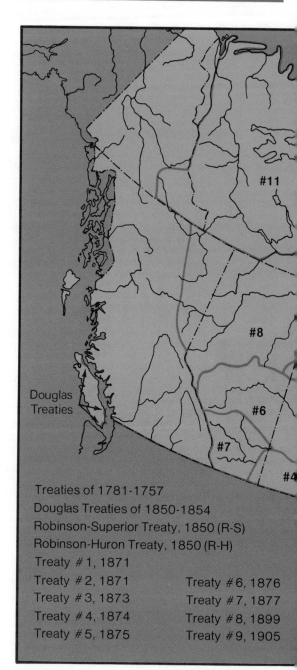

Treaties of 1781-1757
Douglas Treaties of 1850-1854
Robinson-Superior Treaty, 1850 (R-S)
Robinson-Huron Treaty, 1850 (R-H)
Treaty # 1, 1871

Treaty # 2, 1871	Treaty # 6, 1876
Treaty # 3, 1873	Treaty # 7, 1877
Treaty # 4, 1874	Treaty # 8, 1899
Treaty # 5, 1875	Treaty # 9, 1905

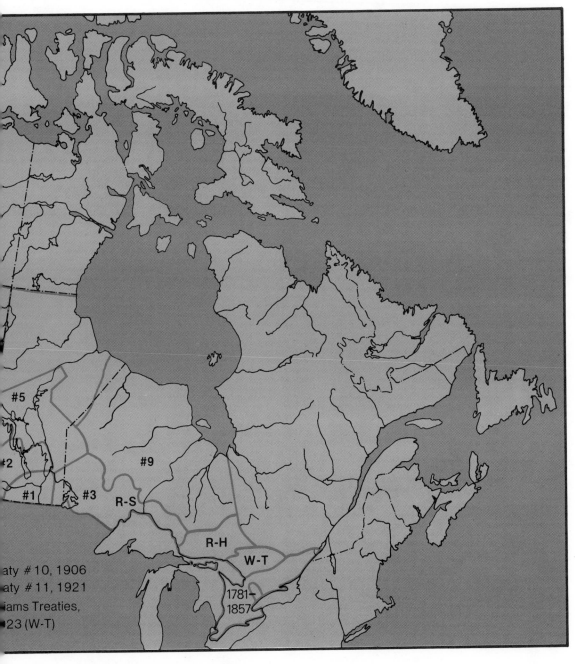

#5

#2

#9

#1 #3 R-S

R-H

W-T

1781–
1857

aty #10, 1906
aty #11, 1921
iams Treaties,
23 (W-T)

Areas Covered by Treaty, 1781-1923

C. W. Jefferys

British settlers. Accordingly, he approached the leaders of a large number of Ottawa and Chippewa people who were living on their ancestral homelands near York (Toronto). He suggested that they move to islands in Georgian Bay.

The native people were probably unaware that they had aboriginal rights in the land. Ignorance of their rights led many of them to accept Bond Head's "offer."

Agreements of this sort were formalized by the Government of Canada after 1870. From then on, native people were encouraged to sign "treaties" to extinguish their aboriginal rights. Treaty law involves extinguishing aboriginal legal rights to the tribe or band's ancestral homeland in exchange for "consideration." What this consideration might be differs from treaty to treaty. In general, the land was exchanged for a smaller tract of land (a reserve) plus some money or goods or both.

In the process, the Indian bands who signed treaties made themselves wards of the Government of Canada. Under the provisions of the British North America Act, the Dominion was made responsible for Indian affairs. Under the provisions of the Indian Act, the native people who signed treaties agreed to an arrangement in which the Government of Canada would assume responsibility for many of their personal and community affairs.

There is much controversy today about the validity of the treaties. Some people now say that a few treaties were forged. Others suggest that the native people did not always know what they were signing when they put their marks on treaties. Thus, in 1973, Mr. Justice Morrow of the Northwest Territorial Court found that there were serious doubts as to whether Indians who had surrendered their lands really understood the terms of the agreements that they had signed. The Court therefore issued a statement which warned governmental authorities that they might soon face challenges from native people wishing to renegotiate the treaties that their ancestors had signed.

Another source of controversy is the matter of whether or not the Government of Canada has honoured the treaties. In the storm of protest that followed Mr. Trudeau's remarks about treaties in 1969, many native people became more aware than ever before of their rights and obligations under the treaties.

> *The honourable gentleman says there is a fraud on the Indians because their food is imperfect. It cannot be fraud because they have no right to that food. They are simply living on the charity of the Canadian Parliament, and beggars should not be choosers.*
>
> Sir John A. Macdonald, 1885

The Question of Illegal Treaties

... it began to become knowledge to an ever growing number of native people that some of the treaties had been forged or were not legal documents for other reasons. Thus, it appeared to them that they were still in possession of their aboriginal legal rights, and they might once again be in a position to negotiate with the Government, but this time on a much more equal footing.

It is not out of the question that such renegotiations will occur. However, the success of such steps is in doubt. One band of native people in New Brunswick found out that a group of non-native people had used forgery to defraud the native people of a large portion of their reserve. The band did not have enough money to take the matter to court. Therefore they assembled their evidence and went directly to Jean Chrétien, who was Minister of Indian Affairs at the time. The Minister agreed that their treaty had not been honoured, and that they had been cheated. However, his only response was to agree with them and tell them that half the land they were entitled to would be returned to them.

If this example gives any indication of the success that native people would have, not just in having the treaties obeyed but in actually renegotiating them, the future does not look bright for them.

Adapted from Scott O. Shields, "The Political Economy of Native Rights in Canada" (Reprinted with permission of the author)

The Indian Act

In addition to aboriginal legal rights and the arrangements agreed to in treaties, there is a third aspect of native people's legal status. It is the *Indian Act*. As we have noted, the British North America Act gives the responsibility for Indians to the Dominion Government. Section 91 of that Act gives the Government of Canada "the exclusive legislative authority" to "make Laws for the Peace, Order, and good Government of Canada with respect to" a variety of subjects, the twenty-fourth being "Indians, and Lands reserved for Indians."

In the absence of Section 91.24 of the B.N.A. Act, there could be no Indian Act, just as there is no Jewish Act, no Baptist Act, and no Blue-Eyed Peoples Act. The Canadian legal heritage does not allow for racial or ethnic discrimination. Our own Bill of Rights and various provincial human rights codes would, except for Section 91.24, disallow the very existence of an Indian Act.

Nevertheless, the Act stands. And it stands today both in defence of and against some very concrete rights of native people. Unlike the ever controversial aboriginal and treaty rights, the Indian Act spells out in black and white over its 56 pages the things which native people may and may not do, as well as the things that the rest of society may and may not do to them.

The term "person" means an individual other than an Indian.

The Indian Act

The Indian Act

The Indian Act is made up of 124 sections. Among other things, it gives the Government of Canada power to control:

- the allotment of reserve lands
- trespass on those lands
- the external sale of things produced on the lands
- the financial responsibilities of the Indian bands
- the administration of wills written by Indians
- the management of money held by Indian bands
- the administration of natural resources found on reserves
- disease control and medical treatment on reserves
- hunting, fishing, and trapping on reserves
- vehicles and traffic on reserves
- pool rooms and "places of amusement" on reserves

In addition, the Indian Act gives the Government of Canada the right to define the local government of native reserves. The Act defines Band Councils and sets up rules for the formation, composition, and powers of Band Councils. It gives the Minister of Indian Affairs the right to dissolve a Band Council. It defines who is an Indian under the law and tells people how they can get out of being Indians if they want to, through a process known as "enfranchisement."

Over all this, the Governor-in-Council reigns supreme. In short, the Minister has the last word over any dispute under the Act, unless people want to undertake costly legal procedures. Clearly, then, the Indians in Canada who are under the Indian Act can be viewed as much wards of the federal Government as "infants and persons of unsound mind" are considered wards of the court. This has been true for more than one hundred years.

Adapted from Scott O. Shields, "The Political Economy of Native Rights in Canada" (Reprinted by permission of the author)

The Indian Act does not apply to all native people. In fact, only about a quarter of Canada's native people fall under it. The people who are defined as Indians under the Indian Act are those who have their names and numbers placed on a list in Ottawa called the *Indian Register.* The Indian Register includes all members of Indian bands, as well as individual Indians, who qualify for Indian *status.* These status Indians include people who are descendants of the native people who signed treaties with the Dominion of Canada.

Needless to say, there were many native people who did not get on the list. First, there are those who never signed a treaty. They and their descendants are *non-status* native people. There are also those whose band or tribe signed a treaty but who were personally absent when the list was made up and never signed the treaty themselves.

Finally, there are many native people who lost their status or gave it up voluntarily. Indian status can be lost by Indian women who marry men who are not status Indians. Not only do the women themselves lose their status, but their children and all their descendants do as well.

What are the benefits of being a status Indian? Until 1960, native people under the Act, besides being subject to the restrictions mentioned earlier, were also refused the right to vote and were forced to carry a "pass" whenever they left the reserve. Most people would resent such treatment, and it would seem that most people would prefer to "enfranchise" — that is, have their names taken off the Indian Register and live as freely as other Canadians. However, the Indian Act has another side to it.

The Indian Act carries with it certain rights. Among the most important are the right to live on a reserve and the right to share in the wealth that might come if any part of the reserve is sold to the Crown. Many native people wished to remain on the Register because that, and that alone, assured them that they would be able to share in the land that was theirs by aboriginal right and guaranteed by treaty.

In addition, the Indian Act provides some positive benefits for many native people. In particular, there are financial benefits. The Indian Act provides exemption from income tax in some cases, and it allows exemption from provincial sales taxes. As well, under the Indian Act, native people have the chance to apply for special government grants for such things as new housing.

Attacks on the Indian Act

Despite the rights and benefits it guarantees, the Indian Act remains a law that most native people dislike. It is a symbol of the "second-class citizenship" that has been created for native people, and it deprives Indians of normal human rights. The Indian Act has been challenged only on specific points. To attack specific parts of the Indian Act only serves to give an impression that the Indian Act in general is valid. As one native leader put it:

> If the Indian Act is not recognized as the main instrument of colonialism in Canada, Indians will continue to attack it in pieces. Removing or lessening some of the worst aspects of the Act will not eliminate the Act itself. This process will only lead one to predict that, for every evil aspect eliminated, a new one will arise to take its place.

Adapted from Waubageshig, *The Only Good Indian* (Toronto: New Press, 1972)

Indians should be regarded as "Citizens Plus"; in addition to the normal rights and duties of citizenship, Indians possess certain additional rights as charter members of the Canadian community.

The Hawthorn Report, 1969

The Indian Act remains in effect. It is disliked by many native people who live under it and by many of the government officials who administer it. Almost everyone would like to see it abandoned or rewritten from start to finish.

There is, of course, a danger for native people if the Indian Act is abruptly withdrawn. Speaking for many native people, the Indian Chiefs of Alberta have firmly rejected the idea that either the treaties or the Indian Act should be done away with. Replying to the Government of Canada's "White Paper" of 1969, the Indians made these points:

To us who are Treaty Indians there is nothing more important than our treaties. . . . The Government must declare that it accepts the treaties.
   The White Paper policy said "that the legislative and constitutional bases for discrimination should be removed." We reject this policy. We say that the recognition of Indian status is essential for justice.
   The White Paper policy says "that those who are furthest behind should be helped most." We do not want different treatment for different tribes. These promises are bribes to get us to accept the rest of the policy. The federal Government is trying to divide us. . . .
   We reject the White Paper proposal that the Indian Act be repealed. It is neither possible nor desirable to eliminate the Indian Act.
   It is essential to review it, but not before the question of the treaties is settled. Some sections can be altered, amended, or deleted readily. Other sections need more careful study, because the Indian Act provided for the Indian people the legal framework that is provided [elsewhere] for other Canadians. Thus the Indian Act is very complicated and cannot simply be burned.

The Indian Chiefs of Alberta, "Citizens Plus" (A position paper prepared for presentation to Prime Minister Trudeau, June, 1970)

Summary

As the Europeans moved steadily westward, it became necessary to come to some arrangement with the native people whose land was being taken.

The native people were organized by the European legal system. Aboriginal legal rights, treaties, and the Indian Act combine to spell out the position of native people in relation to the law of Canada. None of these parts of the law has been interpreted consistently in the interest of native people. Sometimes the benefits that are owed to native people have simply been ignored.

Recently, however, the controversy over native land claims has raised again the question of whether the law has dealt fairly with the native people. Many examples of abuse can be found. However, there is hope that the rights of at least some native people will soon be respected.

CHAPTER FOUR

Contemporary Problems

Many sincere people have talked about the "Indian problem." This phrase seems to suggest that the native people are a problem for non-native society. It could mean, as well, that in contemporary Canada it is the native people who have a problem — that of adjusting to non-native society.

Either one of these positions reflects badly upon the people who hold it. The contemporary problems having to do with native people are neither that native people are a problem for other sectors of Canadian society nor that native people have a unique difficulty in meeting the demands of non-native society. The real problems are those of the *relationships* between native and non-native communities. Such problems cannot be blamed on either group nor solved by either group in isolation.

One of the first problems is that of the image that people in non-native society have of people in native society. Many think about native people in terms of *stereotypes*. A stereotype is a generalized image that we have of another group of people. It is, as American journalist Walter Lippman once said, "a picture in our heads." Stereotypes are attempts to summarize a whole group by a few typical characteristics. Thus, when people talk about the "sentimental Irish" or the "industrious Japanese," they are taking qualities that they think are typical of the group and applying those qualities to all members of the group — as if there were no individual differences.

Howard A. Doughty

> *Don't let anybody tell you anything about the odds against you. Our fathers were fighting greater odds, and if they died and were brave against those odds, you can be brave with these odds. And if you fight, you will at least know what you are fighting today is what they were fighting.*
>
> *Lloyd Roland Caibaiosi*

Stereotypes cause *bias* or *prejudice.* Once a group is stereotyped, people act towards every member of that group in the same way. Stereotypes can make us *biased in favor* of a group or *prejudiced against* it. The manager of a company may try to hire immigrants from countries whose people are stereotyped as being thrifty and hard-working. Behaviour is biased in favour of the whole group, because the stereotype is favourable. Similarly, a negative stereotype can cause prejudice against a whole group of people. These victims of prejudice may be denied equality of access to jobs, housing, and clubs or associations of various kinds.

Historical Attitudes toward Native People

In recent years, there has emerged a demand from natives and non-natives alike that the history of native people be studied from a fresh viewpoint. Instead of regarding native history as something distinct and apart from the general history of Canada, many people have urged the consideration of how native people fit into the history of the Canadian mosaic.

This concern has led to a careful study of non-native images (stereotypes) of native

---

Prejudice in Textbooks

Even the books which people use in schools can display stereotypes. These are a few examples of the image of native people that is conveyed through classroom texts:

In a textbook called *Principles of Electrical Theory,* a diagram to illustrate a principle of force shows an Indian rolling a rock onto a white man's wagon.

A book called *Spelling Mastery 5 . . .* has a picture of Indians shooting and killing a white man driving a wagon train, and pupils are asked to create a story from the picture.

A primary reader, *Out and Away, . . .* shows a child picking up an arrow and saying: "I bet this arrowhead was used to kill a white man."

Says one expert: "This is just thoughtlessness, but it does create an atmosphere of prejudice."

Winnipeg Tribune, October 23, 1972

We believe in dreams, and we believe that people can live a life apart from real life, a life which they can go through in their sleep.
Nalungiaq

people. It has also resulted in an appreciation of why non-natives have not yet come to understand the lives of the native people they have encountered.

> Indians have always been an enigma to white society. Newcomers to North America, from the sixteenth century onwards, were ill-equipped, mentally or psychologically, to understand the temperment of the Indians; nor did they make any real effort to achieve such understanding.
>
> The Europeans who migrated to the new world were concerned with carving out a career or livelihood for themselves, and for most of them this did not include an analysis of the Indian mind or way of life.

R.J. Surtees, "The Changing Image of the Canadian Indian," in D.A. Muise, ed., *Approaches to Native History in Canada* (Ottawa: National Museum of Man, 1977)

The native people were, however, too numerous and too important to ignore. In the early period of exploration and settlement, arrangements had to be made so that native and immigrant peoples could live in the company of one other. The way in which these arrangements were drawn up depended largely upon what sort of image the European officials had of native people at the time.

There have been four dominant images over the years. These can be identified with four major phases in the evolution of Canada since the arrival of the Europeans. The dates roughly correspond to the times during which the image was dominant.

- The Indian as a Noble Savage (1535-1650)

- The Indian as a Warrior (1650-1830)

- The Indian as a Social Nuisance (1830-1960)

- The Indian as a Litigant or Activist (1960-   )

The Noble Savage

To the first Europeans who settled in what is now Canada, native people were stereotyped as *noble savages.* The Europeans were impressed by many characteristics of the native societies of North America. What struck them most was the absence of formal institutions among the natives. There were no jails, no police forces, no deeds to land. There seemed to be no notion of private property; nor was there any apparent government. The native people seemed to live in a "state of nature," untouched and uncorrupted by civil society.

Although they were attracted to this noble image of the native, the Europeans were not much impressed by the native culture. They regarded it as primitive and believed that the Indian peoples would soon abandon their traditions and embrace European values.

The Papal Bull *Sublimus Deus,* as we have already learned, recognized the legal rights of native people. It also emphasized that the Indians were "people" — which meant that they were worthy of becoming Christians. Thus, almost from their first encounter with Europeans, native people were actively encouraged to forsake their ancient ways and take up the new values and beliefs.

It's not just us that we worry about. Our children will be born, and our grandchildren will be born — and they'll have a better world to live in.

Ojibway Warrior, 1974

History of Indian Policy

For the first two centuries of the European presence in Canada, the bases of Indian-white relations (and hence of the white governments' Indian policies) were two: economic and military. The Indians were suppliers of the resources of the country and consumers of European goods. They were also either potential allies and protectors or enemies. The relationship, it should be remarked, was reciprocal; for the Indians usually sought the alliance of the newcomer in their struggles with other Indians and eagerly exchanged the fruits of the country for those of European technology. Fundamental to aboriginal culture was an exchange of presents (usually at repeated intervals) to symbolize the making or maintaining pacts of friendship. In this can be seen the origin of the system of "presents," or treaty payments, which came to characterize the Indian policy of the several colonial governments and their successors.

During the 17th and most of the 18th century, the Indian policy of both the French and British colonial governments was confined principally to attempts to regulate commerce with the Indians — to ensure that the Indians would not attack the European settlements, and to enlist their aid in the American phases of what were essentially European wars. As long as the white population remained small and hence dependent on the natives, relations between Indian and white seemed to be between sovereign powers, although all colonial and European governments held to the principle that the natives were in fact subject peoples, a principle that governed their colonial policies in many other parts of the world. As the numbers of colonists increased, this assertion of European sovereignty over the Indians became open, and gradually the technological superiority of the Europeans ... enabled them to make good this claim.

In the British colonies, where settlement took priority over trade with the Indians, the military aspects of Indian policy predominated over the commercial; and since in 1763 the British conquest of Canada removed France from North America, it was this policy which formed the basis of subsequent dealings with the natives for the next seventy years. The Indian Department, which had first appeared in New York in the 1660s, was concerned primarily with the making of treaties and the distribution of "presents" designed to safeguard settlements and to ensure Indian alliances against the colonies' enemies. It was to be expected, therefore, that the formulation and administration of British Indian policy would be in the hands of military or related authorities. Indian presents, for example, were issued by the army.

Government of Canada, Department of Indian Affairs and Northern Development

> *Indian moneys shall be expended only for the benefit of the Indians or Bands for whose use and benefit in common the moneys are received or held, and subject to this Act the Governor in Council may determine whether any purpose for which moneys are used or are to be used is for the use and benefit of the Band.*

The Indian Act

The Warrior

The *warrior* image dominated as long as the native people were needed to sustain the fur trade or to contribute their military skills to battles among the various European forces, especially battles between the English and the French. The native people were numerous on the frontier. They were accustomed to surviving on the land in spite of great hardship. This made them invaluable as economic and military allies. Their skill at guerrilla warfare (what the French called *"la petite guerre"*) caused them to be invited, in turn, by the French, the English, and the Americans to fight in the eastern woodlands.

The Social Nuisance

As time passed, the native people became less and less important to the Europeans. Then a third image came into the foreground — *the Indian as a social nuisance.* During the period when the fur trade and colonial wars made the native people indispensable to the Europeans, negative images were not allowed to come between the Indians and the whites who used them. However, in places where the native people had ceased to play a crucial role in westward expansion, they lost the esteem they had once enjoyed.

The Europeans had made many promises to the native peoples who helped them. The friendship of the Indians had been won with presents and promises of mutual respect. The British, for example, were fond of assuring the Indians that they were "allies." They would remain "separate nations," yet would benefit from each others' "perpetual protection and friendship."

However, despite all the words and promises, the native people quickly lost their status when they were no longer considered vital to the survival and prosperity of the newcomers. Legally, the native people were placed under the control of the Crown. Their land was taken from them as far as was practical, and their lives came to be regulated by the authorities. The trend throughout the nineteenth century was toward making all native people wards of the Government. The once-feared warrior was reduced to a "social nuisance," a person who would be treated with some compassion, who would be cared for after a fashion, but to whom assistance would be given grudgingly.

Litigants and Activists

More recently, a new image has come to the fore. As native people, particularly in the North, find themselves with a legal right to land on which there are vast resources, they are once again the object of the "white" society's attention. We have already dealt with the legal issues and concerns facing native people. Native people are becoming more and more aware of their rights, and more and more willing to assert them.

It may be unrealistic to assume that the native people will win a fair share of their struggles in the courts and elsewhere. However, the attention being paid to them now is of a different kind from that which has been paid in the past.

Tecumseh

The romantic images of the noble savage and the skillful warrior gave way to a negative image of the native person as irresponsible and often troublesome. Stereotypes were built out of statistics measuring crime, alcoholism, and unemployment. Such stereotypes contributed to prejudice. The prejudice only produced more crime, alcoholism, unemployment, and often suicide. Now, however, no matter how many obstacles continue to face native people, they are no longer easily dismissed.

A Note on Racism

Just inside the main entrance of the Hudson's Bay Company store in Prince Albert, Saskatchewan — a town with many native people in the area — stands a coin-operated machine called "The Indian Scout." A child-size hobby horse rocks when the machine is activated; and, sitting astride the horse, a child uses a pistol to shoot at targets of Indians mounted on a nearby board. Points are awarded on the basis of the child's ability to "shoot the Indians." The Indians in the picture carry no arms or weapons of any sort and are designated simply "Big Chief," "Little Chief," etc. Genocide can be fun!

Akwesasne Notes, Early Winter, 1974

Future Relationships between Native and Non-Native Canadians

Most of Canadian society has come to understand that native people can no longer be ignored. The question now arises: What is to be the future relationship between native people and the rest of the Canadian people?

Conscious efforts are being made to eliminate stereotypes in our society. People are beginning to learn about many of the positive aspects of native society. In particular, native arts have come to be recognized by a wide range of people, from art collectors to members of the general public. However, this kind of activity does not solve all the problems confronted by native people. While many non-native Canadians may show increasingly positive attitudes toward native people, the native people themselves must decide how they are to relate to the rest of Canada.

There are three possible answers to the question of the future relationships between native and non-native communities. Some argue that native people should try to remain separate from the rest of Canadian society *(separatism)*. Others say that native people would be better off abandoning their traditional way of life and joining into the mainstream of modern Canada *(assimilation)*. Still others believe that there is a middle way in which native people would mix to some degree, but would also remain somewhat apart and on their own *(integration)*.

Some beginnings have been made to educate the majority of Canadians about native peoples. However, such efforts must be carefully studied in order to discover whether the pictures they paint of native society are accurate.

Eliminating the Stereotype

No, those who retain the myth of the "noble savage" and talk glowingly about the contributions made by native people to Canadian history may be doing more harm than good. First, they present an unbalanced view of native people. Second, and more important, they tend to make us forget that the struggle of native people is not over. It is not lost in the history of the nineteenth or of the eighteenth century. The struggles of native people are as difficult and as important now as they ever were. This fact can easily be missed when we try to remember native people as we think they were and ignore native people as they are today.

Ralph V. Barrett, "Native People and Industrial Society" (Reprinted by permission of the author)

Education for Native People

What about the education of native people? Schools serve a number of different purposes and teach many different things. Have they been teaching native people to hate their own culture, or have they been teaching in such a way as to instill a sense of dignity in native children? Have they helped native people to acquire skills that are necessary for success in modern society, without teaching disrespect for traditional culture? What has been the record of schools for native people?

There was very little interest in formal education for native people until the arrival of the United Empire Loyalists from the United States in the 1780s, and progress was very slow for a long time after. Nevertheless, a few experiments were attempted.

In 1785, for example, Joseph Brant was able to convince the Imperial Government in London to support a school at Grand River, Ontario. The money came from the military as a reward for the loyalty of native people during the American Revolution. The school was a success, partly because it was administered for a time by native people themselves. Unfortunately, it closed in 1813 as a result of disturbances caused by invading American soldiers during the War of 1812-1814.

A few years later, Joseph Brant visited England to win support for a new native school. In 1824, it opened with twenty-one pupils.

Joseph Brant

Irma Coucill

Then, in 1830, the Company for the Propagation of the Gospel in New England started a manual training centre for native people. The centre was called The Mohawk Institute. It featured a mechanics' shop and facilities for teaching boys carpentry and tailoring. Girls were also admitted, but they were restricted to learning the traditional female skills of weaving and spinning. In 1834, The Mohawk Institute opened a residence. In addition to the day pupils, ten boys and four girls lived at the centre. Later on, instruction in farming was begun. Graduates were settled on small farms near the institute, where the young people could earn a decent living and practice their trades.

Missionaries and some native band councils co-operated to open many more schools for native people. The education was directed as much toward teaching the native children European values as it was toward providing them with practical skills. In 1844, an Ontario government report recommended a detailed plan for the education of native people. The report urged "manual labour schools for the Indians of Ontario. Indian children were to be placed as boarders in such schools, where they could receive instruction in religion as well as in agricultural and other skills."
The conditions under which pupils should be received into the school were also to be made jointly.

The Government retained the right of inspection and the authority to lay down general principles and regulations, and made financial grants for the support of the schools. The religious organization managed the school, contributing part of the funds to its support, and acting as spiritual guide for the Indian pupils.

The policy for a century was to keep native children separate from their own society, and separate from non-native children as well.

Since 1948, some changes have come. It has become the policy of most governments to encourage native children to mix with non-natives. Moreover, in the past thirty years, native bands have assumed more control over schools which are located on reserves. Still, it has only recently been possible for native councils to insist that native children be taught about their own culture and not merely indoctrinated into the values of the larger society.

The residential schools were a source of great resentment among native people, particularly in the West and North. The children would be taken hundreds of miles away from their families and would not see their relatives for months. In an alien environment, pupils would be forced to speak English and punished if they spoke their own language. They were often told that their own culture was barbaric, and they were not allowed to practice their old traditions. In a few cases, there was cruelty and physical brutality. One Indian who had been a resident student in the 1920s told this story:

They starved us up there! We got one egg a year — at Easter. The rest of the time we got dogfood mush (corn meal) and skimmed milk. Those in the staff dining room, though, they got bacon and eggs every day. We never saw fruit from one Christmas to the next, but they sure had it. Why some of those kids just starved to death. One year there were six of 'em died right there at the school ... starved to death!

A. Richard King, *The School at Mopass* (Toronto: Holt, Rinehart and Winston, 1967)

More recently the schools have improved. The people working in them often have the best of intentions and great dedication. Even so, most native students are not being reached. According to the National Indian Brotherhood, only 6 per cent of native people complete high school; the figure for non-native Canadians is 88 per cent.

However, matters are improving. More and more native people are gaining an education. As they do, their influence on their own communities will expand. In some ways, this will mean the further penetration of modern values. In other ways, it may help the native people to take pride in their own culture. Many educated native people have managed to acquire the skills of the European society but have retained a keen interest in their own communities. With a better knowledge of law, politics, economics, and communications, the native young people may be in the best possible position to fight for native rights.

Indian Students Enrolled in Universities Selected Years 1953 to 1971

	1953	1959	1963	1971
1st Year	3	18	25	200
2nd Year	8	12	12	108
3rd Year	1	5	2	67
4th Year	1	4	5	57

Native People and Government

We can learn something about the relationship between native and non-native Canadians by studying the educational system and seeing how it handles the question of native history. What about the relationship between native people and the Government? To learn more about that, it is necessary to study the question of native power (or powerlessness).

Native people who are status Indians have a relationship to the Government of Canada that is clearly stated in the Indian Act. The powers and rights of the Government are so broad that native people can accurately be regarded as wards of the Government. However, does this exhaust the issue? Are there not ways whereby native people can use their strength of numbers to influence government policy?

At first glance, the answer would seem to be "No." Native people, like other Canadians, are incredibly divided among themselves. Common language and customs are absent. Even the values and interests of native communities differ widely. What might be a vital issue to an Inuit in the far North could be a trivial matter to a Haida living in a suburb of Vancouver.

Still, the native people have one thing in common. They have the prejudice of many other Canadians to contend with. They also have the Indian Act. Even native people not presently under the Indian Act may have vital interests in any reform of that law or in any future laws dealing with native people.

Miller Services

O Canada, we know that you are very rich, for you have used our birthright as your very own. We know that you are wise, for you enjoy the respect of the nations of the world. You have boasted that you are just. We must wait a little to see if this is so.

Ernest Benedict

For years, the policy of the Government of Canada was one of benign neglect. As long as the native people did not get in the way of progress, and as long as they did not raise a fuss, non-native Canadians and the Government could fairly well ignore the native people. This attitude has changed. The native people have forced their way onto the political stage.

At the same time, non-native society is eager to exploit the land to which native people have aboriginal legal title. Thus, even native people who would have preferred to remain distant from the rest of Canadian society now have little choice but to confront the issues.

For many native people, involvement with the Government has been frustrating. Even well-intentioned efforts to enforce civil rights have been unsuccessful.

Manitoba Indian Raps Human Rights Laws

Dave Courchene said in a letter to Attorney-General A.H. Mackling that provincial human rights legislation has done nothing for native people.

"After four years, a great deal of time, energy, and headache, I have come to the conclusion that there is nothing we can do in working with your department or its office or its agencies to obtain justice for our people. ... You leave us no alternative now but to look for other methods to fight for the human rights of our people."

Regina *Leader-Post* (October 17, 1972)

On some occasions, those "other methods" included direct political action, sometimes with violence resulting. In August, 1974, the Ojibway Warrior Society occupied Anicinabe Park in Kenora, Ontario. One of the young leaders, Louis Cameron, defended the action this way:

You cannot go into the whiteman's courts and fight for your rights. There you're standing with whitemen, and you're standing with foreigners — you're playing into their kind of game, where they control everything. So this is not a civil right or a legal right. What we are fighting for when we take up arms is for a human right.

Later that summer, about four hundred native people marched on Ottawa and presented a *Manifesto.* They were met by police and forced off the grounds of Parliament.

The burst of anger in the mid-seventies has been replaced by at least a temporary calm. Native people are concentrating on immediate local concerns and are building stronger organizations to meet these concerns in the cities and on the reserves. They are building up strength in their own communities.

In the effort to restore some of the self-confidence and skills of traditional societies, the native people have discovered that they can often get support from the very governments that have long frustrated them. A small example is the administration of criminal justice. Efforts are now being made to develop co-operation between the local communities and outside authorities. Experiments such as this will not solve the major disputes about land claims, but they are extremely valuable in the daily affairs of native people. They may well form the basis of constructive relations between native and non-native society in areas of importance to all.

The Department of Indian Affairs has been making the mistakes for us. We have never had the chance to learn from the mistakes we might have been making.

Henry Jack

Manifesto

We the native Peoples have banded together to come to Ottawa seeking justice.

We the Native Peoples are here to talk about justice. We are here to talk about equality and human rights. We are here to talk about the right of all people to live as free people.

For many years we have received promises instead of human rights. Promises instead of justice. We are here to say the people cannot live on promises.

Our people lived in freedom and harmony with our mother earth thousands of years before the coming of the Europeans and their values. Our people had strong families, our people had education, our people had control of their lives, our people had the religion of giving and respect for all of our mother earth's creations.

Today our people exist in the midst of the Canadian extension of European competitive values. Today our people have alcoholism. Today our people have no education. Today our people have no work. Today our people have no housing. Today our people have no respect.

We are here to talk about violence.

We are against violence. The violence of racism, poverty, economic dependence, alcoholism, land theft and educational warfare. This is the violence that has hurt our people. We say it is time for the democracy of Canada to end its political and social violence against our people.

We say it is time for the Canadian political system to be reasonable and listen to the voice of our community.

We say you have been unreasonable. The proof is evident in the conditions our people exist in. Since the politicians have taken control of our lives the destruction of our communities has increased.

We are here to speak of solutions.

We do not want promises and rhetoric.

We want humane action.

We are here to talk about constructive action.

This time we are still willing to talk but we will not sit idly to the side while the destruction of our people is completed.

We only seek to live as free people. It is the way of the land and its children.

The will of the people to be free is supreme.

The right of the people to be free is divine.

Ontario Services Remote
Indian Communities

Flying in a bush plane has become part of everyday living for people like Dennis Bevilacqua, Probation and Parole Officer in Thunder Bay. Along with two officers from Kenora, and one from Dryden, Ontario, Dennis is responsible for providing probation services to a large section of northern Ontario. Names such as Fort Hope and Pickle Lake Reserve are as familiar to them as Ottawa or Montreal.

For over three years now, travelling courts including judge, Crown Prosecutor and probation officers have been visiting the reserves, dealing with criminal justice problems right in the community. Each trip north involves a three to four day stay in the isolated areas.

As much as possible, offenders are supervised in their home communities, rather than moved south to lock-ups. This has been made possible, according to Dennis, by the fact that most of the communities are "... hiring their own band constables (who) are either from the community or have moved onto the reserve to do the policing. In most of the 25 to 30 communities involved, the travelling probation officers are assisted by part-time probation aides and the band councils on the reserves are also an integral part of the justice process. Some areas do have facilities for overnight detention, but that's only when it's really necessary.

"More and more native people are getting involved in their own communities," notes Dennis. "Band Councils, probation aides and families are all working out solutions for people causing problems. We had a real surprise the last time we held court. Fort Hope asked if, rather than sending people to jail, the offenders could do some necessary work in the community. While it was the chiefs who presented the suggestion, it was a natural idea that came from the community without any prodding."

The travelling court is a real event. "Everybody comes, family and all," observes Dennis. "Every community has someone who can interpret and there isn't a person within a hundred miles who doesn't know what happened in court that afternoon. The chiefs often give presentence reports on the spot. I'm continually amazed by the frankness they express."

New ideas for the prevention of crime are being talked about. "All kinds of suggestions are being tossed around right now. Communities are asking for things like group homes and high schools. One of the major roles I'll be playing in the next little while in terms of education is in letting people know what resources are available.

"The northern supervision program is a means of turning the problem back to the community," observes Dennis. "We're saying, 'You have to look after this individual. This is his home. This is where he's going to live. You can't just ask me to come in and haul him out.' You've got to come up with a solution that is acceptable both to the community and to the individual who's in trouble, so that everybody's problem is solved."

Liaison (Ottawa: Government of Canada, Department of the Solicitor General, December, 1977)

Inuit Art

Dorothy Harley Eber

Inuit artists detail for us home life in tents and igloos, aspects of the hunt, birth and death, and the spectrum of Inuit life. They record beliefs and legends, stories of true events, and, of course, they depict a marvelous diversity of animals and birds.

Most of the artists whose carvings and prints have so thrilled southerners over the last thirty-five years lived, until recently, essentially the same kind of camp life that their ancestors knew for hundreds of years before them. There were some differences, of course. Most hunters used a gun, not bows and arrows; most Inuit gained part of their living from trapping and trading furs for modern goods.

However, although there is much to interest students of different cultures in the Inuit society, there is just as much of interest to students of art. It is not possible to miss the enormous vigour, the sure design, the elegance of form and execution which characterize Inuit art at its best.

Grey Stone Sculpture, by Pauta

The Hunters, by Parr

Man Hunting at Seal Hole

What is the history of Inuit art? The Inuit first came to the Arctic thousands of years ago. They showed skill in the making of tools and clothing. In addition, they made small, fine carvings that may have had magical and religious significance. Later, in the nineteenth century, missionaries and others provided them with pencils and paper for drawing.

After World War II, an incident occurred that sparked an explosion of creativity and produced the sculpture and graphics now known around the world. The writer and artist James Houston, known to the Inuit as "Sowmilk," brought back small stone carvings from a sketching trip he made to Port Harrison in Arctic Quebec. Subsequently, a programme to sponsor the development of art in the north began. It was widely recognised that the Inuit needed a new source of income. The forces of change, sweeping in on their life during the first fifty years of the century, were proceeding at a terrifying pace. For the first time, as the Inuit put it, they have had to "live with money." Out of this necessity has come an art of remarkable quality.

The Hartt Commission

Efforts to develop strategies which will benefit native people economically, politically, and socially are also taking shape through the work of people like Ontario Supreme Court Justice Patrick Hartt. Named head of a Royal Commission on the Northern Environment, Hartt listened carefully to the native people he met. In April, 1978, he produced his first report, a small part of which is reprinted here.

The Need for Co-operation

Recently, a new spirit of pride has arisen among the Indian people. Their new organizations have been formed and have become strong and forceful advocates of change. They seek a new and improved future for the Indian people, which I interpret as involving them in taking over control of their lives, of governing their local affairs, and of gaining a guaranteed access to resources which will give them an economic base on which to build their future.

Their problem, I believe, is largely due to lack of opportunity in the communities, and this lack of opportunity is directly due to the absence of a resource base. Various approaches to ensuring access to resources have been worked out in other provinces faced with northern development pressures. Perhaps the best example is the James Bay Agreement.

Although controversial, it offers one type of local Indian government and a resource access-funding package which is designed to foster a large measure of economic self-sufficiency with an opportunity for preservation of a traditional lifestyle for those who wish it.

One thing is clear: the problem cannot be resolved by the Indians alone, nor by the Indians dealing only with the federal government. Nor do I think the answer is to treat this entire issue as a legal matter and refer any conflicts to the courts; the issue is moral and social as well as legal, and such a broad range of concerns is not best dealt with by the judicial process. Direct discussions among the Indians, federal and provincial governments will be required if meaningful progress is to be made. Such discussions can hopefully smooth the path of change taking place over the next few years, as well as resolve some of the questions which have been raised.

During the hearings, I was encouraged by proposals from both Grand Council Treaty 9 and the federal Minister of Indian Affairs at Moose Factory supporting the concept of tri-partite negotiations. The official position of the Ontario Government did not go so far as this, and tended to rely more heavily on the use of the courts to resolve issues in dispute. I am optimistic, however, that all three parties will see the merit of this approach and give it their support.

The Métis

A separate but related set of problems exists for the Métis and non-status Indians. The Métis are persons of mixed Indian and European ancestry, the progeny of the first contact between the white explorers-traders and the native peoples they encountered. Non-status Indians are persons of Indian ancestry who, for various legal reasons, are not recognized as being Indians (in terms of the Indian Act) by the Government of Canada. Both the Métis and non-status Indians are ineligible for any programs benefiting the Indians and have none of the rights that Indians might have.

There are today some 3500 Métis and non-status Indians living near or north of 50. Because of their Indian ancestry, they find that white society rejects them as equals. They do not share equitably in employment opportunities and wealth. Many are unemployed and are forced into situations which they find degrading and totally unsatisfactory.

For the most part, the Métis and non-status Indians want development and a share in its benefits, but not at any cost. They, too, have a reliance upon the land. Many of them continue to hunt, trap, and fish, which is a lifestyle they share with the status Indian. The Commission was told, however, how the Métis and non-status Indians are often as unwelcome on the reserves as they are in white society. Unlike the status Indians, they do not even have broken treaty promises to support their cry for justice.

The Métis and non-status Indians must not become the forgotten people in attempts to resolve the issues dividing the white and Treaty Indian peoples of the North.

The Basic Problem

In one sense, the position of the native people in the North is illustrative of a general dilemma facing our present society. The nature and structure of that society has the effect of designating as "unneeded" an ever increasing number of people — that trend must be reversed. It is a fundamental function of any truly human society to provide each citizen with an opportunity to contribute meaningfully to that society, and in return be affirmed by it. To accomplish this will involve fundamental conceptual and structural change.

It is my impression from the hearings that many people have a sense that we, as a society, are being propelled in inappropriate directions, but so far there has been a failure to provide any real options. The Indian people have a completely different social and cultural orientation which could provide an important object lesson for the rest of us. Empathetic recognition of what it means to have a different way of looking at and understanding the world could be the first step to a wholly new appreciation of the limitations of our own present consciousness and in the examination of an alternate direction in which society may move.

Hartt Commission Report, April, 1978

One reason for optimism is the fact that the Government of Ontario responded to the Hartt inquiry by making its author the head of a permanent committee to oversee development in the North and ensure that it is beneficial to the native people who live there.

Summary

The position of native people in Canadian society is special. The native people were the first Canadians and, despite the immigration of people from all over the world, the native people have retained their unique identity.

Unfortunately, many people in non-native society are prejudiced against native people. As well, many native people do not want to become completely like other Canadians; they want to keep their culture. This poses several major problems in Canadian life.

There are those who wish to see native people assimilate into the majority of Canadian society. There are others who want to keep native and non-native Canadians strictly apart. Neither extreme is likely. Instead, some form of integration is probable — an integration which will provide native people with all the rights and opportunities of other Canadians, but which will ensure that the special status of native people is not ignored.

CHAPTER FIVE

Native Society in Transition

In this concluding chapter, we will briefly examine the social changes that affect native society. We will also consider the response that native people have had to social change.

We have already talked about the native people of the North. These Inuit are faced with an invasion of "white" technology, institutions, and personnel. They must meet the challenge that confronts them. In one person's view, this challenge is really a trap. Hugh Brody writes:

> Northern development is good because, among other advantages, it gives native people a greater range of choice: they will, with education and industrial advance at the frontier, be able to choose between a life on the land and wage employment.

So far, so good, says this author. However, a closer look reveals that it is no longer possible to live on the land. There are too many people and too few resources. Thus, in the interest of helping the native people, efforts are made to create more jobs. Even greater economic development (which disrupted the traditional society in the first place) is said to be urgently needed, in order to solve the native people's problems. The cure for the illness is more illness:

> With this circular and self-justifying argument, policy-makers effectively narrow down the alternatives: Eskimos must become wage-labourers.

Hugh Brody, *The People's Land* (Markham, Ontario: Penguin Books, 1975)

In the process, basic changes occur in every facet of native life. In the first place, native people who used to live nomadic lives and travel across the Arctic in search of

Public Archives of Canada

game now live in permanent settlements. The life of the settlement is dominated by non-natives, even where natives are a majority of the population.

In the settlements, the native people have been promised a significant voice in local affairs, but there is little evidence that they have been given it. An Inuit woman expressed her resentment in this way:

> Some of the people are still doing whatever the government officials and the white men tell them to do. Maybe that is why government officials think that the people are stupid. . . . I think that in the future this should be done. . . . If the council wants to do something, the people here should just decide to go ahead . . . we should tell the Government to stop coming here, because they are not really trying to help. The people should tell the Government to go away and try to fool people somewhere else.

Quoted in *The People's Land*

But the Government will not go away, and neither will the oil companies and other developers. What is a constructive response to this vicious circle? In the second chapter we examined some of the ideas presented by militant native people. In this chapter, we would like to consider what realistic alternatives are available.

The Urban Indian

Until recently, native people were rarely welcomed in Canadian cities. The Government of Canada seemed intent on a policy of exclusion. So deeply felt was this policy that Indians were not granted the right to vote in federal elections until 1960. However, this policy was intended only for the short term. Native people had always had the right to give up their Indian status in return for the vote. Thus, we must look more closely to see what the federal policy really represented.

In 1868 the Indian Act was "designed to lead the Indian people by degrees to mingle with the white." A government document of the time stated that "the happiest future for the Indian is absorption into the general population, and this is the policy of the Government."

> The apparent contradiction between a policy of assimilation and the maintenance of reserves therefore dissolves. The reserves were meant as forcing grounds for the inculcation of "white" values and religion, until the Indian could be assimilated into the larger society.

Edgar Dosman, *Indians: The Urban Dilemma* (Toronto: McClelland and Stewart, 1972)

The instruments used to develop a programme of "citizen apprenticeship" were varied. We have already discussed education at some length. The schools were designed to keep native children apart from the influence of their homes and families. The Church was influential too. As a government publication stated in 1961:

> The missionaries are a part of the standing army of our Dominion who . . . help to maintain the

Be wise and perservere.

Blackfoot Proverb

peace and prosperity of our land [and] prepare the districts for the advent of the settler. . . . It pays to send the Gospel to the Indians.

The native people are no longer actively discouraged from entering non-native communities. The attractions of the cities are obvious from the native viewpoint as well.

The problems of poverty and unemployment are often coupled with despair and confusion. Thus, one of the major problems facing native people is their social adjustment to the impersonal urban society.

Here, the response of native people has been to establish centres where natives may go for help and counselling. These centres provide some of the best services available to native people. Their continuing growth provides one example of the kind of self-help that native people rely upon. Many believe that the local centres will have to be co-ordinated with large organizations.

Some Native Opinions of City Life

Life on the reserve is too quiet, and there is not enough to do. . . . if I went to a small town where the rent is cheap I would not work as well, because in a small town you really are an Indian.

Some of the people here can't read, but . . . everybody here likes television. I think watching television makes many of the people here know what living in the city is like. When I see life on reserves and then on television, there is no doubt that the city is better.

I like coming to the city. You can really have a good time, but once a year is plenty. I would not want to live here. I just want to be with people I know.

When I came to Toronto, I tried to find my cousin. Every time I would look for him, he would not be at home. When I came here, I thought I could stay with him. Maybe he could help me. But he does not want to help me. He does not want to see me. He thinks he is white.

Mark Nagler, *Indians in the City* (Ottawa: St. Paul University, 1970)

Woodland Indian Art

Bernhard Cinader

In the 1960s, an entirely new artistic development occurred in Northern Ontario. Norval Morrisseau, born at Fort William, began to paint the legends of his people. He first used black ink on brown paper, depicting the spirits and their interaction with people. Later, the subject widened into images which dealt not only with myths but also with his view of the prehistory of his people, their relations among themselves, with nature and with life.

The first attempts of Morrisseau to paint the sacred legends of his people were fiercely resisted by those who guarded the secrets of the Midewewin society. However, Morrisseau persisted; and as he developed his own capacity as a painter, the opposition to his work gradually declined. His influence on other native artists soon made itself felt.

Carl Ray, originally discouraged by the hostility which his drawing evoked, returned to his creative work and began to draw his version of legends and life.

Further south, on Manitoulin Island, Daphne Odjig Beavon and other young painters, still in high school, began to express themselves in drawings and paintings. Their artistic activities were a facet of their growing interest in their heritage.

Conflict between Good and Evil, by Carl Ray

The McMichael Canadian Collection Kleinburg, Ontario

**Tribute to the Great Chiefs of the Past,
by Daphne Odjig**

*The McMichael Canadian Collection
Kleinburg, Ontario*

The History of Native Organization

"Indians," writes Hugh Duplisea, "despite some similarities with other ethnic and 'racial' groups, have a unique place in Canadian history. They merit special attention because they are the original peoples, and because they have retained a special status throughout Canadian history. Native people once possessed all of the land, continue to possess tribally controlled land, and are the inheritors of special treaty rights, promises, and privileges. This condition gives them a distinctive view of themselves and of others."

In the time before the advent of the Europeans, native people lived in many diverse societies. Many native societies displayed complex religious traditions, languages, and governmental arrangements. True, the level of technology and economic development was limited in comparison with modern European society. However, the majority of native communities (and European societies as well) could not simply be lumped together and treated as though they were essentially the same.

The native societies differed among themselves as much as any collection of different tribal or national groupings did. What they came to have in common was the contact with European society and the challenges that such contact brought with it. To understand the present relations between native people and the rest of Canadian society, and to anticipate what may happen in the future, it is important to look at the structure of native organizations in Canada. As individuals, native people may succeed or fail in trying to meet their personal objectives. Only as a group can they succeed in a socially and politically significant way. Among the pioneers in native organization was Chief Joe Capilano of the Squamish people in British Columbia. In 1906, he went to England to petition King Edward VIII. The Squamish people had many complaints, including:

1. Despite promises of compensation, native land title in British Columbia had never been properly extinguished.
2. Whites had settled native lands without permission and against the Indians' wishes.
3. The Government of Canada had ignored the native peoples' protests.
4. Indians were not permitted to vote; nor were they consulted on major issues affecting them.

Capilano's trip was in vain. However, as one writer observed, this was "the beginning of inquiries into the land question." Led by native people who had learned something of western methods, the Indians of British Columbia found a live and clear issue (the land question) upon which they could focus attention.

The first thing to be learned was that the idea of complete assimilation, like the idea of complete separation, is only a theoretical possibility. What actually happens lies somewhere in between. The lives the native people would lead would involve much of the traditional culture and some elements of the western way as well.

This combination of their traditional culture and the new western culture was always changing, and it is continuing to change and be reshaped. It does not deny any continuity with the past; it is rooted in the past. Nobody exposed to the pressure of confrontation with European society could remain the same, but the old culture has not been entirely supplanted. Instead, cultural community patterns are expanded to include new situations.

The Problems of Organizing

The Allied Tribes of British Columbia are a good example of early efforts at organization. They took their case to the Judicial Committee of the Privy Council in England, which at that time was Canada's highest court, and asked to be compensated for their land.

The court demanded that they give up all claim to the land *before* a judgement would be given. Naturally, the native people refused and tried elsewhere. They then appeared before a Special Joint Committee of Parliament, as a first step before going to court. However, in 1927, Parliament declared that the Indians had no claim and told them to stop their demands. In return, they promised $100 000 per year instead of a treaty. This was seen as a defeat, and the Allied Tribes broke up.

The experience taught many lessons. In the years that have followed, native people have organized new groups in the territories, in the provinces, and at the national level. The first organizations were often divided among themselves, unsure of their goals, and short-lived. Among the most difficult problems was

that of religion. Many efforts to build national organizations out of provincial and local groups failed because native people who were Roman Catholic and native people who were Protestant could not work together.

Most often, however, the problems arose because the native people were attempting only to preserve their identity and retain their culture. They seldom thought of applying consistent pressure on non-native society, nor of doing more than protesting some specific injustice.

"Thus," says one analyst, "although they continued to think of themselves as Indians, their stance lacked the militancy and assertiveness which is to be found in some of the Indians today. Not until the last two or three decades have these men and women begun to declare popularly their intention to find an alternative to assimilation."

After World War II, native organizations began to grow and expand. Their ambitions turned from merely local or tribal issues. They began to focus on provincial and national objectives.

Troubles, of course, persisted. They lacked money, grass-roots support, and a sense of general purpose. They tended to be "crisis-oriented." They would spring up in response to a particular problem; but when the problem was resolved, they would disintegrate. As well, there was the question of representation. With a variety of different and competing groups, it was difficult to determine which organization (if any) truly spoke on behalf of the Indian people.

In 1969, the Hawthorn Report stated:

> The nature of Indian organizations has been such that the Indians Affairs Branch (of the Government) and two post-war joint committees of the Senate and House of Commons have been baffled by the difficulty of determining the following of the persons who have claimed to speak for certain groups. In a number of instances, the view presented by one organization . . . was repudiated by a group of Indians for whom the organization claimed to speak.

New Trends

Some efforts have been made to overcome this divisiveness. The National Indian Council was begun in 1961 under the leadership of William Wuttunee, a Cree lawyer from Alberta. The aim of the Council was clear. It was to promote "unity among Indian people, the betterment of people of Indian ancestry in Canada, and a better understanding of the Indian and non-Indian relationship." It tried to involve status and non-status Indians and Métis. It put on exhibitions of native arts and crafts, as well as Indian Princess pageants; and it helped to plan the Indian Pavilion at Expo '67.

By 1971, the Council recognized that it had failed to accomplish its goals. It was run mainly by native people who were comparatively wealthy and who tended to live in the major cities of Canada. Its appeal to poor Indians and native people was limited. Since 1971, the most important organization has been the National Indian Brotherhood. It has co-operated with the provincial associations and has given support to Métis and Inuit causes.

The publication of the White Paper on Indian Affairs, however, brought the greatest unity to Canadian native people. Dave Courchene of the Manitoba Indian Brotherhood declared:

> No single action by any government since Confederation has aroused such a violent reaction from Indian people — never have Indians felt so bitter and frustrated as they do today.

Harold Sappier of the Union of New Brunswick Indians was one of many native leaders who felt the same way:

> The Maliseet and Micmac people of New Brunswick, along with their "blood-brothers" across this country have always made abundantly clear their deep feelings about their aboriginal and treaty rights. We are not going to be swayed by vague assurances.

The solidarity expressed by such leaders is certainly a constructive step towards unity among native people. However, there are still many problems confronting native people who wish to work on their own behalf to obtain justice and develop a way to live in balance with non-native society.

Still, much progress has been made. Many native reserves are now largely administered by local band councils, which promote social and economic programmes. They are augmented by co-operatives and associations for the retailing of consumer goods, and for the development of specific economic projects such as the production of commodities from native crafts to cattle. The native people who need help in cities are aided by a large number of Friendship Centres, which provide social activities and counselling services, and also form a major community centre for people of native ancestry.

The need to bring native claims forward to the political and legal authorities has required more effort. During the last decade, native peoples' organizations have undertaken legal suits and have continually lobbied the governments of the provinces and of Canada. These organizations remain the most well known, and perhaps the most important, native groups in Canada. They have successfully broadened their range of interests from purely local projects and specific complaints to the point where they must now be included in decisions affecting public policy for the entire country. The result has been impressive.

In the nineteen-sixties, for example, even prominent native artists like Buffy Sainte-Marie were permitted to have personal success throughout North America, provided they did not attempt to raise controversial issues.

Native artists and activists are now receiving a hearing. However, there is much left to be accomplished. Perhaps it is best to give the last word to a native person.

Career Obstacles

I've had three major record companies, all of whom were ecstatic on signing me, who then would tell me they'd never, ever, met such resistance trying to get an artist air play. The D.J.'s would all say, we'd love to play Buffy, but. . . .

My concert halls were filled, my reviews were nice, so obviously the press was digging me, but with no air play the press would also say, where have you been? I was being asked to sing at the White House, Nixon's, and asked not to sing certain songs, and I said no, of course, what was the sense of that? Get Olivia Newton-John, or somebody. Johnny Carson was asking me to be on the Tonight Show, and his second-in-command was saying, but of course you will not sing the following songs nor will you talk about the following subjects.

And I was under FBI surveillance. I had one record company look into the situation, and the FBI said, yes, we have quite a file on this person, we have 31 pages on her, and the record company just said, well, we don't want to get involved in that.

You know, it doesn't take long after something like this happens for listeners to forget who you are. It doesn't take long. It only takes about four minutes to hold a person under water, and then they're dead for the rest of their life.

Buffy Sainte-Marie, *Weekend Magazine* (January 14, 1968), p. 6

Indian Goals
Howard Adams

The Indian seeks, as with most Canadians, a real cultural identity. Because we are so oppressed, because our culture has been so eroded and distorted, our search for identity is so urgent. In our schools we are taught to believe we are shy, retiring, and lacking self-confidence. This brain-washing deprives us of our leadership qualities.

Indians should not condemn white society, but should recognize it and deal with it. Indians should be able to hire their own teachers and control their own reserves. The Indian language should be used at all official meetings on the reserves. If a white government official comes there, an interpreter should be brought along.

Indians should promote their own culture and language. But the problem is that the true history of Canada's Indians has never been written.

Summary

To accomplish the goals of native people, the rest of Canadian society must be prepared to respond favourably to the demands which native people are now making. While the economic development of Canada depends in part upon the rational use of the abundant natural resources on and in the land, the rights of native people must also be considered.

Few native people wish to halt progress. However, many native leaders are stressing that economic progress should not be achieved at the expense of native people. They are building their own organizations to look after native communities everywhere. They are also urging the rest of Canada to become involved in a plan for economic development which will not waste our resources or sell them cheaply, which will build jobs for all Canadians, and which will deal fairly with the native people who live on the land that is to be exploited.

Fair treatment includes just payment for the land, the creation of jobs for those who wish them, and the protection of the environment for those who wish to combine wage and salary employment with traditional ways.

GLOSSARY

Band   A specific group of native people who are officially registered as members of that group. Although a band is usually identified with specific reserve land, a significant percentage of band members do not live on the land reserved for their band.

Band list   A list of the names of every person who is a member of a band and is entitled to be registered in that band.

British North America Act   An act of Parliament which established Canada as a dominion within the British Empire. Under Section 91 of the Act, the Government of Canada was given exclusive authority to make laws with respect to native people.

General list   A list of names of all persons who are not members of a band but are entitled to be registered.

Indian   A person who, pursuant to the Indian Act, is registered as an Indian or is entitled to be registered as an Indian.

Indian Act   A legislative attempt on the part of the Government of Canada to bring together and articulate the responsibilities it inherited from the British colonial government through its treaties with the native people and through sub-section 24 of Section 91 of the B.N.A. Act.

Indian register   A collection of band lists and general lists in which the name of every person who is entitled to be registered as an Indian is recorded. This register is maintained by the Department of Indian Affairs and Northern Development.

Métis   A word which originally applied to people of mixed French and native ancestry. It is now used to refer to people of combined native and non-native parents or more distant ancestors.

Non-status Indians   Indians who are native by birth and heritage, but who are not classified as "Indian" under the terms of the Indian Act.

Reserves   Tracts of land set aside through agreements or treaties for the exclusive use of specific bands of native people. Reserve land is crown land held in trust for the band. Individual band members can never have a clear title to their property on the reserve but can obtain "exclusive user rights" through a "location ticket." Location tickets can be sold or given only to registered members of the band that owns the reserve.

Status (registered) Indians   Indians who are classified as "Indian" under the terms of the Indian Act. The two terms "status Indian" and "registered Indian" are used almost interchangeably. However, the term "status" should only be used to designate a native person who has treaty status.

INDEX